buftn blch 2008

BLAZIN' BLOATS & COWS ON FIRE!

By
Baxter Black

Illustrated by
Bob Black
Don Gill
Dave Holl
Charlie Marsh

COYOTE COWBOY COMPANY
BENSON, ARIZONA 2006

All poems written by Baxter Black
Copyright © 2006 by Baxter Black

Published by: **Coyote Cowboy Company**
P.O. Box 2190
Benson, Arizona 85602
All rights reserved

Cover design by Becky Harvey

LIBRARY OF CONGRESS CATALOGING IN PUBLICATION DATA
Main entry under:
Cowboy Poetry
Bibliography: p
1. Blazin' Bloats & Cows on FIRE!
2. Cowboy-Poetry
3. Poetry-Cowboy
4. Humor-Cowboy
5. Agriculture-Poetic Comment

I. Black, Baxter, 1945-

Library of Congress #2006904328
ISBN-13: 978-0-939343-49-2
ISBN-10: 0-939343-49-5

OTHER BOOKS BY BAXTER

THE COWBOY AND HIS DOG © 1980
A RIDER, A ROPER AND A HECK'UVA WINDMILL MAN © 1982
ON THE EDGE OF COMMON SENSE, THE BEST SO FAR © 1983
DOC, WHILE YER HERE © 1984
BUCKAROO HISTORY © 1985
COYOTE COWBOY POETRY © 1986
CROUTONS ON A COW PIE © 1988
THE BUCKSKIN MARE © 1989
COWBOY STANDARD TIME © 1990
CROUTONS ON A COW PIE, VOL 2 © 1992
HEY, COWBOY, WANNA GET LUCKY? © 1994 *(Crown Publishing, Inc.)*
DUNNY AND THE DUCK © 1994
COW ATTACK © 1996
CACTUS TRACKS AND COWBOY PHILOSOPHY © 1997
(Crown Publishing, Inc.)
LOOSE COW PARTY © 1998
A COWFUL OF COWBOY POETRY © 2000
HORSESHOES, COWSOCKS AND DUCKFEET © 2002
(Crown Publishing, Inc.)
AG MAN the COMIC BOOK © 2003
HEY, COWGIRL, NEED A RIDE? © 2005
(Crown Publishing, Inc.)

FORWARD

Welcome to another guided tour of my world. As I travel back and forth across the country I pick up your stories like a horsetail picks up cockle burrs, like your velvet pants pick up dog hair, like a lotto winner attracts a million new friends!

As I repeat often, "I don't have to make this stuff up!" The truth underlying these stories is their appeal. It's the truth in humor that makes it funny (that's why there's no science fiction jokes). "That happened to me!" I hear said over and over.

How many different ways can a cowboy or rancher or farmer or veterinarian get bucked off, bit, stomped, run over, butted, stepped on, spit on, pooped on, gored, pummeled, pounded, dragged, snagged, flogged, bogged, plowed down, kicked up, pitched off, bowled over, punched out, scraped, lacerated, lamed, lumped, bumped, flattened, rolled, hammered, humped and humiliated? The answer: Apparently more than the number of stars in the sky!

How I wound up making a living entertaining the agricultural masses is still a mystery to me. I don't think about it except to appreciate my good fortune and not take those of you who like my stuff for granted.

I hope this book is up to snuff. If it's not, just return the unused portion of the book and I'll return the unused portion of your money!

Many thanks once again, to the Bucarangelos; Buckaroo/Michelangelos whose illustrations make my book eminently more enjoyable. Without them I'd just be another Homer without The Odyssey, Pablo without the Picasso, or Lemon without the Meringue! And one last thank you to you wonderful folks that keep me from needing to find honest work! I couldn't do it without you.

In conclusion I would like to dedicate this book to my mother and Grandpa Tommy who have lived their lives, born their tragedies, appreciated their good times, and served endlessly to make the world a better place for those around them.

They are a part of who I am . . . the best part.

TABLE OF CONTENTS

A GOOD HORSE...36
A HORSE MATTERS..35
ALPACAS AND CHICKENS..120
ANATOMY OF A WRECK...34
ANIMAL SIMILES...18
ANVIL AND THE TELEPHONE POLE.................................40
AUCTION BARN MIRACLE...69
AVIAN FLU FOBIA..64
BEHIND THOSE EYES...109
BIG ONE THAT GOT AWAY BLUES.................................122
BLAZIN BLOATS...8
BOAT ROPING..41
BUFFALO TRADING..62
CALVING MISDIAGNOSIS...58
CEMENT POUR..59
CHICKEN HOUSE ATTACK...44
CHICKEN TRAINING...82
CONTEST OF WILLS...54
COUNTRY TRUCK CITY TRUCK.....................................91
COW DANCING..71
COWBOY EMERGENCY ROOM..80
COWBOY NEEDS A COW...16
COWBOY VOCABULARY MISCONCEPTIONS.............................50
COWBOYS ADVICE TO THE LOVELORN...............................15
CRIPPLE CREEK CALVIN AND THE SNAKEY MARE.....................46
DEFINITION OF A COWBOY.......................................74
DOGS COLUMN..48
ELK SCENT...116
EQUINE EGO...39
FAITH IN CHRISTMAS...90
FUZZY SLIPPER..22
GENERATIONAL DIFFERENCES....................................121
GO CATCH MY HORSE..32
GOOSE BUMPS...117
GRANDPA S WISDOM OF THE AGES................................110
HEY COWGIRL, NEED A RIDE?....................................68
HIGH HORNED RED COW S CALF...................................75
IMMORTAL BRANDING..56
IMPROVING MY HORSEMANSHIP....................................23
JOHNNY THE MULE MAN REVISITED................................96
KELLEY AND THE SUPER COWBOY..................................55
KELLY S HALLOWEEN...106
LAZARUS AND THE OWL...114

LEBKUCHENS ON THE TRAIL..104
LITTLEST SHEPHERD.. 88
MACHO SURGERY.. 29
MASTERCARD - PRICELESS..113
MULE CONVERSION..94
MULES ARE PECULIAR... 28
NINE LIVES OF A SHEEP...86
OLD WAYS DIE HARD..65
ONE LEG UP...81
OUT THERE... 66
PAWN SHOP PINUP GIRL.. 102
PENNSYLVANIA SHEEP DOCTOR..60
PETTING ZOO...70
POOR MAN'S RANCH RODEO...26
REUNION OF THOSE WHO DARED...108
RING BUYING...101
ROLLING ROUND BALES... 98
SALMON MOUSSE...112
SIXTY FOOT ROPE... 6
SO LUCKY TO BE AN AMERICAN...124
STORY OF THE COWMAN AND THE COW................................. 78
TAKE YOUR BELONGINGS AND GO....................................... 118
TAXIDERMY HEIFER... 19
TEN REASONS TO BE IN THE SHEEP BUSINESS.......................87
THESE BOOTS.. 100
TILT TABLE VS ROPING... 76
TURKEY'S THOUGHTS AT THANKSGIVING.............................97
TURTLE AND THE RABBIT... 84
UTAH COWBOY.. 17
WANDA AND THE WILD HEIFER... 52
WHY AMERICA NEEDS COWBOYS.. 12
WHY THE HORSE..38
WOMEN AND HORSES...24
WOMEN WEARING CHAPS...14

THE SIXTY FOOT ROPE

I was in Guadalajara, Mexico one time and this man was selling rawhide ropes. He shook out a loop tall as his head, did the houlihan flop, threw that sucker across the freeway and caught a taco vendor on the other side!

"How long is that rope?" I asked.

"Catorce brazadas," he said, which meant 84 feet long!

I've always had a fear of carrying such a long rope. Nowdays I have occasion to be in the company of some good cowboys who carry a sixty foot rope. I'm not sure why, maybe it's just because . . . they can!

Last December we gathered my cows and calves into the big trap to wean and ship. One big black steer kept turning back. There was me, Jack Post and Francisco Lopez. That steer finally charged right between us, went right out through my good two-strand bob wire fence, took the balface heifer and the red high horn cow with him!

Well, we're shippin'! So we break out our ropes and take after them.

The country in that part of Arizona is a sequence of mesquite filled arroyos interrupted by rocky ridges. Jack takes after the balface heifer. I figger I better go with him 'cause Jack's older.

The heifer had little nubbins 'bout an inch long stickin' out the side of her head. Jack roped her around the horns!

I looked to the south and there's Francisco chasing the big steer up the next ridge. They were silhouetted against the low winter sun and looked like one of those metal carvings over the top of a Texas driveway. That steer had his tail stickin' straight up in the air. Francisco was right behind him closing the gap. He is grand to watch rope. When he throws, it's like he's cracking a whip.

He threw a beautiful loop . . . and missed! That steer took a hard right down into the arroyo and was crashing through the mesquite straight towards me!

I had my little 35 foot secondhand team ropin' trade-in shook out. I was ready, my horse was ready, we were standing on six tiptoes! The steer came up out of that arroyo like a dirt bike comin' over a jump!

For a microsecond our eyes met. We became one. I could see him thinking . . . should I turn left? Should I turn right? He came straight at me! From six feet I threw my loop . . . and caught him . . . going by me . . . the opposite direction . . . at the speed of beef!

I'm trying to catch my dallies and he's tearing them out of my hand like he's falling off a cliff! Thank goodness, 'cause if I'd caught one, I'd been jerked over backward and smashed flat!

Ten minutes later I am on my hands and knees at the bottom of the arroyo, under a mesquite thicket, holding on to this horse who would go home if I let him, and I could never get within two feet of the end of my rope!

All of a sudden I had a vision. Like Saul on the road to Damascus. The light shone down upon me and I said, "THIS IS WHY THEY CARRY A SIXTY FOOT ROPE!"

It takes a long time to learn to be a cowboy.

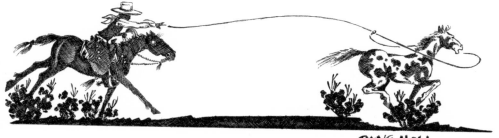

DAVE HOLL

BLAZIN' BLOATS

I am a student of the cow. When I go out to check my cows, I'm mostly tryin' to find them! And when I do, I don't just ride by and wave, I ride up as close as I can get.

Note: Range cows are kinda like K-Mart employees, you can't actually walk up to one. You see them at the end of the aisle, you run down to catch them and when you get there, they're gone! I tell people they are domesticated, not tame.

So, whether it's a pair or a bunch of 'em, I sit there and check 'em out. And I like to think, that is the high point of that cow's day! Cows lead a fairly boring life; they graze. And when they're not grazing, they are laying around chewing their CUD.

This cud is part of a magnificent digestive mechanism that allows cows to utilize fibrous vegetative material that is otherwise completely indigestible by simple stomached animals like people. For instance, cows can derive nutritional benefit from lettuce! Who'd a thunk it! People eat lettuce because it's the next best thing to eating nothing. If you wanna lose weight, the best way to lose weight is to eat (fill in the blank).
No! Nothing! But nobody wants to eat nothing, so they eat lettuce, which is the next best thing.

This cud is swallowed and descends into the rumen, a vast fermentation vat, which is very big and is filled with nasty green liquid and swallowed cuds. From a veterinarian's point of view, if you get it on you you've gotta sleep with your hand hanging off the bed for 3 or 4 days! These cuds take a number, like at the motor vehicle department and line up to get regurgitated. So the feed is chewed, swallowed, regurgitated and re-chewed until it cries uncle and gives up its nutrients.

One of the by-products of this digestive process is that cows give off enormous quantities of carbon dioxide and methane. Horse people are aware that the horse's exhaust is at the rear...cows don't do that. Cows belch off the gas. It is a great system unless or until something goes awry, i.e., an occlusion of the esophagus or a diminution in the motility of the rumen and it creates BLOAT!

Yes, bloat. For those who did not take ruminant physiology in middle school, sometimes when you're driving down a country road and you pass a group of cows in a pastoral setting grazing, you may notice one of them appears more turgid than the others, sort of football shaped. And when you look closely her feet are actually levitating slightly above the ground.

I am certain this occurs because sometimes when I'm trying to find a cow and I'm on a fresh track, suddenly, the track disappears! I remind myself . . . don't forget to look up.

Suffice it to say that bloat can be a life-threatening situation. Cattlemen and veterinarians are prepared for such emergencies. We have a delicate surgical instrument called the BLOAT HOSE! Think of the stack on a Kenworth, which is passed down their esophagus until it hits the gas *pocket in the rumen and a gush of fetid rumen breath escapes, relieving the pressure.*

But, say you're on your way to church and you don't have your bloat hose in your purse, you might be carrying the handy trocar! It is a sharpened screwdriver inside a sleeve. The trocar is stabbed into the left flank that is pooched out, through the half inch of skin into the rumen, the screwdriver is pulled out, the sleeve remains and the gas escapes and you save their life.

But there are those occasions when one is caught completely unawares, as in the following poem.

"My gosh! How'd you set yer hat on fire?
Snorting gunpowder again?"
"Well, I didn't do it on purpose," he said,
Rubbing the spot on his chin.

His eyebrows were singed off uneven
And unsymmetrically skewed
While the glass was gone from his glasses
Which rendered him spectaclely nude.

"It was dark," he said, "You know methane will burn?
Me and Jake were out checkin' the stock.
We were comin' in late and found one
That looked like she needed the doc.

But we were both cow paramedics
Trained to do more than just ride
And savvied her dire situation
All bloated and laid on her side.

Not having a bloat hose or trocar,
First choices for saving her life,
I blindly palpated the left flank
For the place where I'd plunge in my knife.

I inserted the tip of my dagger,
It fit like a key in a latch
When Jake said, "Here let me help you!"
With a flourish the fool struck a match.

A blue flame roared out of the orifice
Like St. Helens come back from the dead!
A whoosh, like an airbag exploding
Pinned my ears back to my head!

I thought I'd been struck by lightning,
St. Peter was trimmin' my jibs
And was callin' me home with my boots on
Smellin' like barbecued ribs!

Poor Jake took the blast a full frontal
Though his moustache protected his lips,
When he took his hat off of his bald head,
He looked like a partial eclipse.

What kept us from burning too badly,
Or at least to me it makes sense,
Was the fireball of flammable gasses
Was mixed with the rumen contents.

The flames quickly waned to a flicker.
The cow was now layin' plum flat.
My chest was all greenish and sticky
. . . I could see by the light of my hat.

But the insult that cut me most deeply
Was not the burnt hat or the blood,
My mouth had been opened in protest!
And I found I was chewing her cud!"

WHY AMERICA NEEDS COWBOYS

1. So the press will know how to describe people who don't mind taking the handoff and running over the middle on a '4th down and one.'

2. To prevent the abuse of facilities, i.e., corrals, calf chutes, barb wire, aluminum gates, telephone poles, old car bodies, split rails, or electric fence. When properly placed, the cowboy can be sandwiched between these inanimate objects and the cow, to soften the blow and lessen the damage.

3. To serve as one of the few sources of amusement in the life of a cow.

4. To serve as an example of a job description that is routinely excluded from such actuary lists as'most dangerous,' 'lowest paid,' 'longest hours,' and 'life expectancy' because they can't afford insurance anyway. I mean, who would insure a boot jack, a plastic whip, or a rubber hubcap hammer.

5. To stand as a reminder of what you can become if you don't do well in math, English or study hall.

6. There will always be a need for laboratory rats in experiments examining the chaos theory, Murphy's Law and, what is loosely called 'Job's affliction.'

7. To act as a buckle bunny magnet.

8. To serve as inspiration for all the Charlie Russell, Roy Rogers, and Louis L'Amour wannabees.

9. To prove that no matter how good you are at somethin', you can always get bucked off!

10. To show that being a male chauvinist pig doesn't pay...well.

11. To shine as an icon of truth, justice and the cowboy way.

12. To lend credence to the belief that underneath that stoic romantic image painted on the silver screen is a simple human being with feet of cow manure.

13. And finally, the world needs cowboys for the same reason we need knights, punt returners, banjo players and Marines. You have to have someone you can send in first.

WOMEN WEARING CHAPS

There's something oh, so charming about girls basketball
Or lawyers wearing pantyhose or sweethearts with a drawl
I like doctors with mascara and with painted fingernails
And flirty flight attendants with their pretty ponytails
There's school marms in the classroom, some are nice but some are meanies
And hurricanes named Rita and there's models in bikinis
I like pilots wearing lipstick, flying flappers flexing flaps
But in my heart my greatest love is women wearing chaps.

Oh, I know what you are thinking, 'That's the dumbest thing I've heard'
But a cowboy's life is simple, so it's really not absurd
See, all day he's punchin' cattle and, though some might not agree,
One can tire of endless blue skies and the vast serenity
Of the majesty of mountains and the beauty of the plains
That the western singers yearn for in their wistful sad refrains
But for me the scene I picture 'tween the daydreams and the naps
Is ridin' drag on my ol' pony behind women wearing chaps

You can call me a romantic, even pansy if you choose
It's not the cowboy image that the movie moguls use
But, beauty's in the eye of the beholder, so we're told
A flower to a botanist, a fungi to a mold
Tight jowls and big firm hineys is a pork producer's dream
Clear water to a plumber, to a vampire it's a fleam
But, to a cowboy makin' long days checkin' fence and water gaps,
His idea of perfection
His triple decker, shoot the moon, till death doth he collapse
His Venus on the half shell is a woman wearing chaps

Photo by Jessica Brandi Lifland ©2006

14

COWBOYS ADVICE TO THE LOVELORN

While entertaining the Farm Bureau in Ventura, California, I was introduced to three cowboys who were colluding on a column with the editor of The Ventura County Star. It is called "The Luv Wranglers," an advice column for the lovelorn ala "Dear Abby." They gave me a couple of examples, the first and last listed here. They inspired the others. I was proud to be in their company.

Dear Saddle Trio, My wife wants a divorce but still insists on us going to a marriage counselor, so she can say she tried. What should I do?
Signed, In-The-Crosshairs
Dear Crosshairs - Change states.

Dear Triple Tie-Down Triad, I'm a 22 year-old ex-model, now bank Vice-President with a new Dodge dually, 3 horse slant, ranchette with roping arena, and 4 credit cards. How can I get my surfing boyfriend to pop the question? Signed, Palamino Yearning
Dear Yearning - Kiss your surfing smoothie goodbye, and send a copy of your resume, complete with a picture of the Dodge dually to:
thetritipcowboys@rightonbaby.com

Dear Tumbleweed Triage, Our first wedding anniversary is coming up soon and I'd like to get a gift for my wonderful cowboy hubby that will be thoughtful, sweet and demonstrative of my love for him that will last through the ages. Signed, Still Swooning
Dear Swooning - Beer is always a good choice.

Dear Tripe-eating Triplets, I'd like to marry my cowboy, Robert, and have proposed to him in a poem, which I can't quite finish. Can you help me? It begins:
"I'll marry you, I'm ready, Bob,
If you'll just get a steady ..." Signed, Anxious in Oxnard
Dear Anxious – Sorry; nothing comes to mind.

Dear Triangular Trailriders, My cowboy has been out in the wagon and I haven't seen him for six weeks. Any ideas for what I might wear for our first night back together? Signed, Stars in Her Eyes
Dear Stars - Barbecue sauce

Dear Triplicating Cowpunchers,
What's the best way to get a guy to commit?
Signed, Desperately Seeking
Dear Desperately - Commit to what?

A COWBOY NEEDS A COW

A cowboy needs a bovine like a sailor needs a plank
Like a blister needs a toe hold, like a robber needs a bank.
A cowboy needs a cow brute like a pack mule needs a crup
Like a stuntman needs an actor, like a catcher needs a cup.

A cowboy, friends, without a cow is moon without the Earth,
As macho and heroic as a whithpered lithper's curth.
See, cowboys need a dogie like Quasimoto needs a hunch,
Like a redneck needs a beer can just to have something to scrunch.

I say a cowboy needs a cow, they're joined at the hip.
Politicians and reporters have the same relationship
Without each other to torment, they don't know where to start.
Like criminals and lawyers, you can't tell them apart!

So, to those who think I'm whining, that I'm pitiful and sad,
That I'm just another loser throwing good love after bad,
It's not all that one-sided, as I've learned in therapy,
'Cause my cow finally admitted that she really needed me.

DAVE HOLL

16

THE UTAH COWBOY

He was a Utah cowboy and he wore a black felt hat
That was pulled down level to his ears till the tops of them were flat.
The weathered lines upon his face showed he had a checkered past
I reached to shake his proffered hand but both his wrists were in a cast!

"Carpal tunnel?" I asked deadpan but he never broke a grin.
"Rodeo," he quietly said. "Bulls or broncs?" I asked again.
"No. Team roping," was his answer. I responded, "Quite a wreck?"
"Well, the heeler saw it better," then he winced and stretched his neck

And then began his tragic tale, "I was on my trader horse
Who hadn't bucked for ne'r two weeks and was steady on the course.
You know how you have always thought if yer dallied up and tight,
A horse can't buck while draggin' all that weight? Well, pardner, that
ain't RIGHT!

"My heeler's horse came off the ground when my pony broke in two!
The second jump we cleared the fence but I held my dallies true.
The third time like a slingshot put the poor ol' steer in orbit
And I'm thinkin', 'If I make this ride I might get a good score,' but

He fired me from the saddle with such force he come unshod,
And bucked so hard up to the sky, so high that I saw God."
Brigham Young was there beside him, according to this spiel,
Respectfully I waited for the wisdom he'd reveal;

Some divine sent revelation of man's purpose here on Earth,
Or a glimpse of cowboy heaven, or what angels' cows are worth.
"Did he give you any inkling of your future, dirt to dirt?"
"Yes, he did," the cowboy whispered, "He said, 'Son, this is gonna hurt."

ANIMAL SIMILES

Animals have many uses. Traditionally, they are discussed as to their purpose; i.e., a source of meat, milk, or as a beast of burden. Other categories include, as a pet, as a show steer or dog, or possibly as an object of worship like Free Willy.

But one of the most significant ways in which animals have contributed to the civilization of mankind is as a simile or metaphor; strong as a lion, graceful as a gazelle, sly as a fox, crazy as a loon, nosy as an elephant, cute as a bug's ear. Certain animals convey feeling; gentle as a kitten, mad as a hatter, fat as a tick, slicker than silk pajamas on a garter snake.

Plant life also offers itself up as subjects for metaphor and simile, but plants never seem to have the same dramatic effect; they fought like apples and oranges! Quit squashing around! A jello mold in the hand is worth two in the bush! What's good for the kumquat is good for the kudzu! The Trojan radish! The kelp whisperer! The dandelion king! See? Flora just lacks the zip that fauna can deliver.

There are those times in our lives when we are surprised, insulted, derided or kidded, and we need the perfect animal rejoinder, unfortunately the attacker walks away with a smirk because we couldn't think of one. Snappy animal comebacks are useful in the category of 'damning with faint praise.' I offer these examples for your consideration:
Smart as: a trainload of sheep,
        a wheelbarrow of turkeys,
        a busload of animal crackers, or,
        a bucket of night crawlers.

Or...Witty as a team of oxen, charming as a fruit bat, clever as a cedar stump, cuddly as a centipede, ethical as a congress of millers, regular as a three-toed sloth, deep as a housefly's thoughts, loyal as a fruit salad, welcome as head lice, romantic as a hippo's kiss, and handy as wings on a liver fluke!

See how much nicer animal similes are than just saying, "Sometimes Baxter's dumber than boiled gravel."

TAXIDERMY HEIFER

Unlike some other veterinary specialties, when a new food animal graduate makes a farm call, the odds are that the cow man knows a lot more about what's wrong with his cow than the ingenue veterinarian.

It's no shame, it's just the way it is. It also explains why a large portion of veterinarians move on after their first year of practice so their mistakes don't cling to them for years as they practice around the community.

But it does make the point that cattlemen know a great deal about the animals in their care and are capable of handling most situations themselves.

So it is presumed that when I make a farm call for a calving difficulty, I'm fairly certain I will not be the first one to have my hands inside that cow! The cowman will have already tried to pull it and couldn't. If it was easy he wouldn't have called me.

Suffice it to say, I don't save them all. Which leads me to my diversified practice possibilities.

As the only local cow vet, I had calved a lot of heifers
And as such was most reluctant to keep score
'Cause no matter how I tried and tried, I couldn't save them all
So on the side I opened up a taxidermy store.

"Stuff yer heifer," was my motto, it was on my business cards.
And the message I recorded on the phone
Said, "If I can't save her, you can! As a conversation piece.
Have her mounted or just standing there alone."

I stuffed them in positions that I thought might catch the eye
One leg upraised her milking on a tire
Or rearing up like Trigger, or with X's on her eyes
Surrounded by a priest and candles waiting to expire.

There were action poses in the stance of how she last appeared
Like on her back, a huge midline incision
Or standing with the calf half out, feet first, the hind legs showing
That looked like some real bad rear end collision!

Or head down in the charging mode, about to mow you down,
The water bag a timeless counterweight.
Or half a mount, just the backside, with my OB chains protruding
As I last saw her going out the gate.

The market for my HEIFERS-IN-DISTRESS grew leaps and bounds,
My cuddly cows kept flying out the doors.
People put them on the mantle, people placed them on the lawn
Like pink flamingos grazing on all fours.

Until, alas, some thought they saw conflict going on
'tween my practice and my taxidermy shop.
"These charges pain me deeply," I told my vet technician,
"My reputations's always been the top.

"What makes them think I'd compromise my veterinary work
To make a little money on the side?"
"Well, they might be misinterpreting your heifer calving price," she said.
"Not many charge a hundred dollars . . . and the hide."

THE FUZZY SLIPPER

Some blamed the incident on her fuzzy slippers.

Brenda is a top hand, and like many ranch women, is especially good at calving heifers. Because of her skill and stamina she and her husband, Perry had synchronized 110 first-calf heifers to calve within a two-week period. Of course, when they bred them they didn't anticipate those two weeks would fall in a period of clear skies and 40 below zero.

She kept two horses saddled in the barn, each on a twelve hour shift. She checked the heifer lot night and day, almost hourly, nipping back in the warm house for a bite or a nap. She would slip off her cap, Carhartt coveralls and boots, then dive under the electric blanket. She slept in what she wore under the Carhartts, a tee shirt and underwear – 'granny' underwear, she described it, Hanes Her Way, 3 in a pack for $2.00, she got at Wal-Mart in Bismarck.

By the second week she was a zombie. During one particularly cold night she woke, dressed and walked to the corral. She noticed as she mounted her horse that she was still wearing her fuzzy pink slippers. "So what," her frozen jaw muscles mumbled.

Riding into the heifer lot she found a new baby steaming in the frigid air. Brenda slid a loop around his hind legs, swung to the saddle and began skidding him across hard ground toward the calving jugs in the barn. Mama followed. As she passed through the gate, something went wrong. The calf's feet went to the inside of the post, the rope to the outside, snagging it in a perfect V. It stopped the horse; he swiveled in his borium shoes to the left, snugged the rope up under his tail, and threw a fit! Brenda pitched her slack, grabbed at the horn, reared back and pointed her fuzzy-clad toes in a sort of "Michelin Man imitates Gjermunson."

The horse continued to buck as the 35 foot rope snaked itself free, steaming, writhing and throwing smoke from under the horse's tail, not unlike an 800-lb marlin, sounding, and taking the line back from Ernest Hemmingway's whining reel!

Brenda came out over the front onto, and into the ice and snow and frozen poop. She careened, luge-like into a snow bank, her fuzzy slippers disappearing and the handy openings on the side of the Carhartts, packing themselves with snow, from her granny's to her sockless ankles.

Back in the living room Perry was sympathetic, "He's never bucked before," he said, "It must have been the fuzzy slippers."

The following fall one of the guilty slippers was found in a coyote den two miles from the house by a pheasant hunter. Bet there's a story behind this, he thought, bound to be.

IMPROVING MY HORSEMANSHIP

I consider myself as progressive as any horseman when it comes to considering techniques and devices for improving my horse's welfare or my horsemanship. Horse magazines are packed with testimonials and advertisements for all manner of horse improvement, supplies, seminars and secrets.

Humans have been riding horses for millennia and everything we take for granted today was once the brainstorm of some Mongolian or jolly old English knight's trainer.

"I don't know Cedric ..... When I heft my lance, it pulls me over and I fall off."

"Funny, Sir Lancelot, I was just reading, in the Camelot Horseman about a new piece of gear invented by a team roper in western Wales called a steer up, I'll check into it."

You would think after centuries of marketing geniuses trying to sell a horseman one more thing, that we would have run out of ideas. I must have 25 different versions of hoof picks laying around; homemade, artistic, crude, sharp, shiny, worthless, fancy, functional and farrier approved.

I've bought stirrup swivels, knot eliminators, metal hondas, automatic gate openers, sweat less saddle pads, fly masks, cribbing devices, fence climbers, freeze brands, magic minerals and special secret supplements...my latest; "A unique hoof support system for the farrier, horse owner and veterinarian." A lightweight fiberglass unit with an interchangeable foot cradle and straight post. It has magnets to hold rasps, nippers, clinchers, etc.

Actually I like it! It replaces three 'hoof support systems' I'm using now made of disc blades, 2 inch pipe, tire tread, and cotter keys, each weighing more than a good sized mastiff!

At a fair in Kanab I bought a patented stirrup extender for my neighbor Jack. He's got a little age and not of tall stature so mounting involves parking his horse next to a cut bank, water trough or hay bale. We installed the stirrup extender on his saddle which lowers the left stirrup a full three inches "with a push of a button."

Three days later I asked Jack how his new stirrup extender was working. "Great," he said. "But there's one complication, I can get my foot in the stirrup okay but when I try and swing my leg over the saddle, I fork too soon!"

WOMEN AND HORSES

I've always thought that one is either a horse person or is not. It is evident even in little children. You hold them up to a horse's head, some children immediately reach out to pet it and others draw away. It is a level of comfort and trust that is noticed by the horse as well.

More girls than boys, to my observation, naturally relate to the mind inside the horse's head. I often have to explain to boys that there is no mechanical linkage, no steering column, set of cogs, hydraulic brake lines or transmission gears that connect their rein hand to the horse's feet.

Within five minutes of jumping on a horse's back for the first time, boys will be yelling and showing you how they can "make it run." Then they jump off and walk away like they've just driven a go-cart around the track and parked it. Girls seem to grasp more easily the concept that the reins, heels and body position are signals from a human brain to an animal brain.

So, according to my observation, you would think that the mainstay, the customer base of the explosion of horse whisperer clinics would be men; male horsepersons who want to learn what seems to come naturally to female horsepersons.

But it's not. It is women who will follow a favorite horse whisperer around the country for years, still trying to become "one" with their horse.

Maybe motherly instinct is involved, like a mom still telling her 46 year-old son to keep his elbows off the table and chew with his mouth closed. Maybe she needs the attention and it's cheaper than a psychiatrist. Maybe it's a search for perfection. Or maybe she doesn't rope, punch cows, steeplechase or play polo and horse whisper clinicking is her hobby. After all, the horse might be her best friend, and who better to spend the weekend with.

For you men, I appreciate there are many of you who are horse people and, like me, enjoy the clinics. And for you ladies who like to ride, but could give a rat's pantaloons for the touchy-feely aspects they promote, I acknowledge the multitude of exceptions to my observations.

But I can't tell you how many times I've eavesdropped on horses talking to each other at the ranch, in dude string corrals, at training clinics, riding clubs, gymkhanas and horse shows, and the phrase I hear repeated o'er and o'er is, "...Oh, I don't know. She just understands me better."

DAVEHOLL

25

POOR MAN'S RANCH RODEO

The working ranch rodeos are enjoying a resurgence around the country. They allow ranches to enter teams and compete against cowboys from other ranches. They are often well organized and can be pretty fancy events.

This has caused a minor disgruntlement among ranchers who, though officially qualified for the Working Ranch Cowboys Association based on cow numbers and full time employment, don't have the finances to hire full time help.

Tracy explained, in their case the neighbors all try to schedule their work together and hope nobody gets busted up, too bad. She says the concept of a four-man team isn't usually in the cards. If she and her husband can even get the banker or the town derelict for half a day they consider themselves in tall cotton.

Team penning consists of the two of them, halfway mounted, in a wire pen with two hundred Brangus cow and their bawlin' calves. It involves lots of yelling and dust.

Nor, she said, does team doctoring resemble the official ranch rodeo event. If she's alone and finds a sick one in the pasture she sorts the (a) loco'd (b) pinkeye'd (c) prolapsed (d) all of the above, heifer off and prods or chases it a jillion miles to the pens, or if she and her husband are together he ropes the beast and she runs down the rope to inject the critter without getting clothslined, head butted, kicked or stabbing herself!

The winter olympics version involves roping afoot in slushy snow and cowboy water skiing. The WRCA branding is the closest to the real thing on her ranch, except if you rope more than two by the neck you spend the rest of the day on the ground mugging.

Wild cow milking is a favorite event of many ranch rodeo fans. On Tracy's place they do most of their wild cow milking in the squeeze chute on a rank, bad bagged, big titted fightin' cow that was supposed to have been sold last fall except she came up bred and a couple of perfectly sound, good-tempered ones didn't. The hardest part is getting the witch back in the chute four days in a row till the calf can suck.

She said she does enjoy the saddle bronc and the wild horse race events. But only to watch. They haven't started green colts on their ranch since they raised their insurance deductible to $45,000.00. The last ranch rodeo that she and her neighbors combined to enter featured a saddled steer riding. *(not a contest that seems destined for perpetuity, author's note)* A bunch of Corriente roping steers are turned out. The roper rides out ahorseback, ropes a steer, team members saddle it and ride across the finish line *(although I can understand the cowboy mentality that invented such a great event, author)* In Tracy's team's case, when two-hundred pound Fred swung aboard the corriente it sank to the ground and became boneless as a sleeping hound dog.

I don't know if we will ever see a professional rodeo association that truly represents the cow business as Tracy lives it. But it's possible. After all, this is how we got women's mud rassling, Bowling for Dollars and reality programming on TV.

MULES ARE PECULIAR

Mules are peculiar. First, they're not real. They are the equivalent of a Caterpillar body on a Volkswagen chassis, with Cadillac suspension, a Cummins diesel and lawn mower wheels. Not to mention two dish antennae and a rear window wiper. So it is no wonder that people who are attracted to mules, are peculiar in their own right.

And, just like the animals they admire, mule people are proud of their "uniqueness." I'm not sure how to characterize this condition but I once described Bishop, California's Mule Days as, "like a cowboy poetry gathering, only more intellectual."

Yes, mules seem to have an intelligence that horses do not. This is demonstrated by their traits of not overeating grain if given the chance, not panicking in a tangle, and pooping in designated areas (which they have tried to teach the horse, who only half heartedly, or half hockily, have adopted).

Mules, unlike horses, also play by the rules. Often their rules, but they always color within the lines. During Hurricane Floyd of 1999, the coastal plains of North Carolina was hit hard. Torrential rain followed by massive flooding occurred. Huge sections of the flat plain were underwater. Dale and Jim had their property inundated. They had salvaged what they could from the house and led their four mules out to the road in knee-deep water toward safety.

The mules balked at the property line. Dale's "house rules" forbade the mules to cross that imaginary obstacle. They freed the mules, thinking when the water got high enough, they'd find a way out. But next morning the mules were back in the barn and the water was up to their backs. Jim haltered the boss mule and tied him to the transom of a 16-foot boat with a 25 horsepower Evinrude. They putted out toward the road. The mule came right along until he reached the edge of the property. He dug in all four feet and stopped the parade.

Jim was twistin' the throttle and fishtailin', but goin' nowhere. Then surely but steadily, Boss mule backed clear to the barn towing the sputtering ship like he was reeling in a 400-lb catfish.

But mules do like to have fun. Jackson Hole Jerry had a big mule that liked to stand in the back of his little two-horse trailer. Jerry came home one day to find the trailer at the bottom of the slope below the house. "Who moved the trailer?" he asked his wife. "Not me." she said. Jerry hooked up and pulled it back to the top of the field. He unhooked, started for the house and looked back to find his big mule clomping into the trailer. The tongue lifted off the ground and down the hill he went.

Jerry thought he heard him laughing!

MACHO SURGERY

In the community of doctors of veterinary medicine there exists an elite level. A specialty, that above all others, commands an awe, a respect normally reserved for monarchs. It is the Equine Practitioner.

There is a mystique that surrounds them. Picture the regal equine veterinarian driving through the Kentucky bluegrass country in his silver Porsche Boxter on the way to Walmac Farms to examine Son of Aladar, who is worth more than the GNP of India.

The doctor is met in the yard by an assistant who takes his coat and black bag, garbs him in a sparkling crisp smock, and offers a handiwipe to freshen up. At the barn, the stainless steel table and white drop cloth have been stationed conveniently. Atop, carefully placed, are the gold-plated stethoscope, monogrammed rectal thermometer, and hand-forged antique combination fleam and hoof pick.

Apart from the other specialities this super DVM is treated like royalty. There is no dog hair on their sleeve, no faint aroma of cat urine surrounding their person, no flecks of cow manure in their hair, no piece of placenta dangling from their ear.

The doctor begins imperiously giving instructions, "Walk the horse please." "Trot the horse please." "I would like to see his teeth, thank you." "I would like to see his bill of sale, Thank Yooou!" It's as if they carry the royal DNA and wear the mantle passed down from ancient equine sorcerers.

There still remain many equine veterinary procedures that survive from the time of Sir Galahad and jousting knights. An age when sedatives and anesthetics were not available and practitioners had to do things the hard way.

Some of the procedures still linger on, kept alive by tradition and the need to prove one is worthy of the title, Equine Specialist.

There's a practice in a practice of a vet who works on horses
That embodies the machismo of their kind.
I was taught this ancient practice, the standing horse castration,
Meaning, both he and I were standing at the time.

To cognize the difficulty, the mule-headedness required
To pursue this task of surgery and cunning
One must grasp its deeper meaning. It's often been compared
To changing fan belts with the engine running

Or standing on a bar stool taking bets from one and all
You can stick your head up through the ceiling fan
And never touch a single blade, or spill a drop of beer
The epitome of every cultured man

As a student I remember Doctor Voss's demonstration
As he strode up to the stallion's heaving flank,
"Hold him tight!" he told the helpers who were
hanging on the head,
"He can hurt ya", this stud was really rank,

He tried to bite the halter man but only caught his collar
And slung him to the ground with such a force
His underwear turned inside out! "This is the chosen method
To reduce the chance of injuring the horse."

"You will notice," Doc proceeded, "That I grasp and pull down firmly.
Some resist," (Really? I reckon I would, too!)
With syringe and anesthetic he injected both the cords
Then, finished, backed away a step or two

"Now we wait." "Obviously," said a student in the back who knew it all,
"To allow the Lidocaine to take effect."
Dr. Voss looked at him blankly."No, so you can quit your shaking
Long enough to go ahead and testisect!"

Less you think this macho culture is confined to men alone
I remind you lady vets now rule the world
And a veterinary practice that might specialize in equine
Can easily be run by boy or girl.

And I can personally attest that cutting horses standing
Is a gender neutral practice in vet med.
Cause last weekend Doctor Nancy examined my old pony
And I saw the ceiling fan scars on her head!

GO CATCH MY HORSE

In the old days I resigned myself that bad luck came in threes, i.e., three flat tires, three smashed fingers or three social faux pas. It s com forting to know that good ol Dakota Mike is still proving my theory. And, I m not even counting the initial injury that resulted in a swollen right knee which put him down for a solid week.

It was very bad timing, since he was calving heifers and was very particular about tagging and vaccinating newborns and kept meticulous records. His darling wife fed before and after her town job but couldn t do the horseback heifer check. But she did notice the hole in the wire fence had allowed some mixing. Dakota Mike paced in place and fretted until Saturday when she could help him catch up.

With her help, he saddled Forrest, a bay mustang plow horse cross they named after Forrest Gump. He was big and gentle but not a quick learner. She rode Pony. Mike loaded his saddlebag with tags, vaccine and syringes. He figgered he could pack the nearly empty spindle of barbwire. Darlin would carry the fence stretcher and pliers. He stood on the tie pile to mount. Wincing, he got his right leg swung over the saddle and gently maneuvered his tennis shoed foot into the right stirrup. He squared up and eased Forrest up beside the pickup where he had preplaced the wire roll.

He reached down with his right hand and picked up the wire. The loose roll made a queer rattling sound. One that Forrest recognized from the rattlesnake program on the Discovery Channel. He hunched and fired straight back with both hind legs! Mike had his left hand outstretched with the reins, his right hand outstretched with the wire, his left foot in the stirrup, and his noodle right leg hanging limp. In the time it took him to realize he should drop the wire and grab the horn, Forrest had punched him into a two point landing under Pony s feet. Darlin leaned over and asked, Are you alright? Go catch my horse, he said, palpating his scraped forehead and sore right shoulder.

With the fence repaired, they rode into the heifers. Mike prided himself on his cows mothering instinct. He creaked off his horse, noting the nearby mama cow pawing the ground, and quietly snuck up on a still wet newborn with loaded ear tagger and syringe. He carefully dropped down on the calf with one knee. In a blinding flash he was flying back wards banging his head on the frozen cowpies and filling his collar with muck.

Are you alright? Darlin asked. Go catch my horse, he said.

Across the pasture he again detached himself from Forrest and ap proached another newborn. Not seeing the mother, he managed to strad dle this one and was supporting it between his trembling limbs. He felt something in his crotch and looked down. A black nose and muzzle the exact size and width of a cow s head protruded between his legs. In less time than he could put two and two together, he was catapulted in a flailing arc ten feet in front of the calf and had somehow managed to ear tag his left pant leg.

   "Are you alright?" Darlin' asked.   "Go..." he grunted.

   "I know," she said, "I know."

ANATOMY OF A WRECK

It just goes to show you how quickly a walk in the park can turn into a 4-alarm stampede. The only thing that kept the wreck from resulting in permanent damage to man or beast, was that the soil on the plains of eastern Colorado is loose and sandy.

Paddy, not his real name, and a couple of neighbors were moving some of his cows from one big pasture to the next. Things were going smoothly, the cows knew the way, the sun was shining, the grass was still holding up good, and what could go wrong?

Paddy was riding his big gray gelding. The kinda horse that can do it all. Even the horse was whistling a tune. Suddenly a dingy heifer broke out of the bunch and turned back. She caught the drovers off guard, squirted between them and headed back where she'd come from. The ball of twine began to unravel.

Paddy whirled the big gray and in two jumps they were flyin' across the plain. The crew watching could see Paddy and the heifer appear and disappear up and down across the rolling grass prairie. Gray overtook the heifer and they headed back in the direction of the still plodding herd. The big horse was feeling his oats and had built up a head of steam. The heifer pounded down a sandy ridge past the watching cowboys, followed by horse and rider. Midway down the side Gray stuck his front feet in the loose dirt and exploded! He seemed to stand straight up on his front legs; imagine a pole vaulter, a medieval catapult or stepping on a sand rake.

Very few bronc riders could have stayed on and Paddy was not one of them. There was a scream like someone falling off a cliff, followed by what might have been a giant zipper being opened, a whip cracking, two thuds, a whoomp and a crumple.

Old Gray regained his feet, unhurt. Ten feet away Paddy appeared to be standing on his head, shirt down around his shoulders, boots sticking up in the air and completely pantless! He keeled over like a felled tree.

During the cleanup they deduced that when Paddy was ejected he must have hung his belt buckle on the saddlehorn, because his jeans were torn completely off his body. It took two of them to pull his hat back off his nose and a set of wire cutters to get the sagebrush out of his ear.

The lady who told me the story was an artist but she'd never been able to paint the picture. She said she couldn't ever get the flames just right.

A HORSE MATTERS

I like living someplace where a horse matters.

There is just some country where horseback is the only way to get the job done. Places where the four-wheeler is a poor second, not to mention a noisy, track-leaving unnatural conveyance. Besides, it's hard to throw a rope from.

Helicopters can spot and scare, if that's what you need, but it's helpless when you have to doctor a calf. It is a great feeling to be pushing a cow out of a mesquite thicket, packing a dude down the Grand Canyon or tracking a mountain lion on a high ridge, knowing you're on the perfect tool for the job. You look at a horse different when he's on the payroll.

I like being a person to whom a horse matters.

It puts me in such good company, Robert E. Lee, Teddy Roosevelt, Rudyard Kipling, Ray Hunt, Queen Elizabeth, Jerry Diaz, Casey Tibbs, cowboys, Mongols, Gauchos, teamsters, leppazaners and vaqueros of all kinds. Granted being a horse person doesn't make me easier to get along with, better at spelling, or richer, it simply gives me a direct connection to one of the most ancient, mutually beneficial interspecies relationships on the planet.

Winston Churchill said, "There is something about the outside of a horse, that is good for the inside of a man."

I like being there when a horse matters.

When you can't do the job alone; a cow in the bog, a race against time, a boulder to move, a detour to take, a mountain to cross, a crevasse to leap, a war to win, a sweetheart to impress, or...when you've gone too far to walk back.

Shakespeare's King Richard III said when fate hung in the balance, "A horse! A horse! My kingdom for a horse!"

I've also come to believe that you either <u>are</u> a horse person or you <u>aren't</u>. Many who <u>are</u>, never know it because they never have the chance. It's a primitive acceptance, often mutual. A lack of fear. You see it in some children when they are first introduced to the horse. It always gives me a sense of wonder to be there and help them make their acquaintance. I believe the horse can sense the child's innate trust. It is the beginning of a natural bond.

I count myself very lucky that I get to be a part of the wonderful world of horse sweat, soft noses, close calls and twilight on the trail.

I like living a life where a horse matters.

A GOOD HORSE

He spent his last year living a horse's dream, being loved by a little girl.

A $400 dental bill at age 25 extended his life. I've owned many horses, he's the only one I've ever buried on my place. His greatest trait was that he had try.

"He was hard and tough and wiry, just the sort that won't say die..." was how Banjo Paterson put it in **The Man From Snowy River**.

He made a good cowman out of my daughter, won her a buckle in the team penning. He never placed in the halter class, always a little over-weight, a might short. I took a lot of hoorahin' from the well-mounted boys at the roping arena.

"But still so slight and weedy, one would doubt his power to stay and the old man said, 'that horse will never do...' ibid.

But after runnin' 20 steers he was still bursting out of the box, givin' his all, while the other boys were changin' horses or skippin' turns. And solid? Let me tell ya, even with my horseshoeing skills he stayed sound. Every time I'd buy another horse, and like I said I bought many, he'd become my backup.

"He wasn't my best but he was my ace." McWhorter, Blackdraught.

He was 13 when we bought him. He'd done ranch work and become a Little Britches all around. When he was 17 he took my son for his first ride at age 0.

"A kid's horse needs a cool head. And with wise ol' Skeeter between their knees they was safe as if in their own beds." McMahan, Skeeter

At age 22 he moved to the ranch with us and started checkin' cows in the brush and rocks. My nephews and nieces and tenderfoot friends were his students. Never a plug, boss at the bunk, a voracious eater, he finally wore down. Despite the dental work and soft feed, his muscles melted away. But his spirit remained. That's when we found him a little girl. She weighed less than a saddle and block of salt. He stumbled a little at the trot but she looked like a rodeo queen on his back.

"...To see a fine lady upon a white horse..." Ride a Cockhorse Anon

Now he's gone. Died in the night. Just quit breathin'.

"Amigo my friend, so true to the end
Eras buen caballo, amigo my friend." Buffham and Fleming – Amigo

I said a few words over him. Now I've got to go tell the kids.

WHY THE HORSE?

Why the horse? It's like asking why the sun? Why the heart? Why the color purple? If there were a monarchy, the horse would be king.

Equidae hold an exalted position in the society of mankind. On their backs humans become a better species. No matter how you stack up other domesticated animals, none has quite the stature of the horse. Perhaps it is because of the inherent wildness that is always lurking behind their eyes. It is a quality that is shared with cats. Regardless of how tame or trustworthy, the potential for a feral reaction that can maim or destroy lies within their power.

Horses have always possessed the potential for heroism. Thunderous poetry like *The Man From Snowy River* to *East is East and West is West* elevates the horse to mythical proportions. I grant there are many examples of dogs saving the day, but dogs have become too domesticated, too subservient.

Indians had dogs for millennia and never invented the wheel. Coronado gave them the horse and they became warriors. Ask any handicapped kid what it feels like to be ahorseback. Until the catapult, it was as close as man could come to flying. Muscles contract and explode beneath you sweeping you forward like an eagle over the surface of the earth.

Without the horse the cowboy becomes a herder, Napoleon is infantry, and taxation without representation becomes the sport of kings. The horse is both masculine and feminine. What other animal can be said to prance? Strength and beauty, Beauty and the Beast, hard as horses hooves - soft as a filly's nose! That mare can buck, that stud's a beauty. Like women wearing chaps.

They let us glimpse design perfection, like a cheetah, a linebacker, or a Dodge Viper with blood pumping through its hydraulic veins. Artists strive to portray their power, grace and dexterity. They try to capture their spirit.

Dead run/stop action photo; 1200 pounds balanced on one toe, fetlock extended, nostrils flaring, neck reaching, ears back, mane flying, tail flowing, eyes locked on target and a human attached like a space shuttle to a rocket! It's no wonder they take our breath away.

The horse, more than all other domesticated beasts demands respect. They possess an intelligence that derives from being both predator and prey, hard and soft, brave and skittish, loyal and wary. They may deign to show some affection, but they don't pant and lick. Horses are, after all, royalty.

For that reason I would propose that we eliminate the term "Giddy up". Can you imagine walking up behind Queen Elizabeth or Ghenghis Kahn and saying, "Giddy up."

EQUINE EGO

I was in a western store when a gentleman stepped up to the counter and asked me which cap that he was holding looked better. I asked if he was a baseball player, a member of a rap group or was a corn farmer. He said none of the above, he was a horseman. I said, "Follow me," and escorted him to the man behind the bench, shaping hats.

"Please show this fine pilgrim how he looks in a cowboy hat," I requested of the hat man. The buyer protested. I explained that wearing a good hat was a matter of pride. He said modestly, "Well, I'm not a very good cowboy, I just own a couple of horses. A cap is good enough for me."

"I didn't mean your pride," I explained, "I meant the horse's!"

Horses are dignified animals. Lookin' good is one of the things they do well, and they know it. You don't see many horses in casual wear by choice. Unlike most other animals, they have majestic ancestors as role models. They are the creatures legends are made of. Can you think of another animal who could have been substituted to save the day for The Man from Snowy River, the Lone Ranger, Coronado, Robert E. Lee, Sir Lancelot or Sitting Bull?

No, they've tried camels, donkeys, elephants, even ostriches, unfortunately these beasts usually wind up as comic sidekicks. But when a hero needs a ride, he rides a horse. Pegasus, Sea Biscuit, Fury, Traveler, Champion, Trigger, Silver and Midnight. And the horse is expected to live up to this grand image. These expectations explain the quirks in horses' personalities; stubbornness, stupid habits, flightiness, overeating. They are insecure and must constantly be reassured.

Brushing, new shoes, nice tack, riders with good taste. The whole western wear industry of designer saddles and brand name jeans is fabricated to make the horse look good.

So, for my shabby horseman friend who didn't think he was qualified to "dress the part" by wearing a real hat, you can see the damage he might be doing to his horse's self-esteem.

It's like putting the bridle on over the halter. Do you think the horse doesn't notice? It's like wearing your underwear outside your pants.

So do your part, good horseman, remember, in riding, just like in cooking, presentation is half the meal.

THE ANVIL AND THE TELEPHONE POLE

Sometimes a cowboy will ride a good lookin' bad horse for longer than it makes sense. This flawed thinking may have a more universal application; i.e., hangin' on to a pickup, dog or girlfriend long after they've bit you or konked out.

It's even worse when the injured party thinks he can make a good horse, dog or wife out of a pretty renegade.

Roy was a California cowboy and an experienced horseman. Out of respect, the boss had given him the big, fancy 3-year-old bay to use in his string. He was a green broke, cinchy, snorty and antsy but he looked so good in his white stockings and star.

Within two weeks he pitched Roy into the rocks and broke his arm. But...he was a good lookin' devil so Roy turned him into the horse pasture while his arm healed. Every day Roy would see the bay grazing or kickin' up his heels, livin' the life of Trigger. This injustice began to prey on Roy. He himself couldn't throw a saddle over a horse or cut his own chicken fried steak. All he could do was hand things to the chore boy.

Still, he was a trainer at heart and believed he could gentle the young horse down. One afternoon he caught the horse up and with the help of one of the boys, saddled him...not to ride, just to do some ground-work. Behind the hay shed was a dilapidated board corral that would serve as a round pen. Roy, using a plastic whip, put the pony doin' circles. But the horse was so skittish he would race away, then stop, whirl and generally act like he had iron fillings in his gyro compass. To steady his gait and add some drag, Roy decided to attach an anchor. He got the boys to bring the shoein' anvil out to the corral. He then tied it to the saddle on a ten foot leash and cracked the whip!

The first thing Roy noticed was "an anvil is not near as heavy when it's off the ground!" The horse was racing around the pen, the anvil bouncing, whacking and whip lashing behind the frightened beast! Big pieces of old board and rotten post filled the air like a wood chipper! It sounded like a 747 crashing in a Redwood forest! Roy stood frozen in the center, plastic whip limp in his good arm, as the board corral disintegrated around him.

When the big bay left the corral, the stirrups were bangin' together over the top of his back and the anvil was in midair! It took the boys an hour to saddle up and track him. They found him five miles down the road. He had been subdued by a telephone pole. There were three dallys around the pole and the anvil hung chest high.

Of course, the bay looked no worse for wear. He was pickin' at the weeds around the pole. Roy, however, was another story.

THE BOAT ROPING

As a poet I strive for good solid rhymes. It is my observation that the poems written over the ages that have climbed out of the book to be quoted at churches and campfires, bars and funerals, and at reunions and grade schools, have solid meter and real rhymes.

It's not that prose is not good writing. It's just that it's hard to memorize. You can't just turn to someone sitting next to you in the fishing boat and say, "Here, let me read you something from Chaucer...hold my bait."

But when you can recite The Cremation of Sam McGee to your kid in the hunting tent after you've turned off the Coleman lantern, you get a small taste of the magic that poetry creates.

But perfect rhymes are not easily won, as you can see in this story.

If God intended cows to swim, He'd given them all flippers.
You rarely see a mermaid calf or Holstein skinny dippers.
But in their battle to survive, I've seen cows come unraveled
And to escape the cowboy's loop will choose the path less traveled.

Now Randy wasn't brilliant, but he was a heavy breather,
Which helps when chasin' wild cows who aren't that brilliant either.
To try and even up the odds he called his neighbor Steven
One cow versus two cowboys intellectually's 'bout even.

The cow in question spotted them, stuck her tail in the air
And lit out for the tank dam in the pasture yonder there.
Randy fell in hot pursuit whilst shakin' a big loop out.
He knew he had to catch her quick or his horse and him would poop out.

She led him round the tank dam circumnavigating right
So Steve went round the other way to cut her off in flight.
Please picture if you will the scene, two jousting knights converging,
A loco'd cow between the two, collision courses merging.

She hit the bank, took one big leap and dove in like a porpoise.
The last thing our two cowboys saw was a disappearing orifice.
She swam out to the middle where her feet could still touch bottom,
Submerged there in the water looking vaguely hippopottom.

"We've got her now!" cried Randy as he bailed off his hoss,
And jumped into a rowboat that was tethered in the moss.
He grabbed an oar and cast away and started paddling wildly
And rowed himself out toward the cow who watched him crocodildly.

He roped her off the starboard and half hitched her to the bowsprit.
But...she breached just like a marlin and covered him with...
Sorry, I couldn't come up with a rhyme for bowsprit.
He planned to tow her backwards but her feet dug in the sea floor
And pulled him clear across the pond and out upon the lee shore.

"Abandon ship you lunatic!" Steve yelled above the racket.
"I can't!" he cried, "I left my life vest in my other jacket!"
The hull was flyin' all apart, and headed for a shipwreck,
The poop deck lived up to its name, or should that be cow-chip-deck?

Great big pieces crashed and cratered scaring fish and water fowl.
Seals barked, catfish mewed, I even heard an otter growl.
But he hung on there behind the cow despite the flying shrapnel,
No doubt to go down with his ship like any good ship cap'n'l.

Long story short Steve's horse rebelled and pitched him where it's stickery.
He watched the cow and rowboat disappearing in the hickory
With Randy still connected like the tail of a comet
Most probably feeling seasick but without the time to think about it.

A piece of keel between two oak trees snagged 'em like an anchor,
Stopped 'em like a hangman's rope, capsized the ship and sank'er.
The cow had Randy up a tree, up there in all his glory
As she butted up against the trunk and marked her territory.

"Pretty scary," hollered Stevo, "I'm surprised you wasn't drownded!"
"That cow just plain outfoxed me," muttered Randy, then expounded
"But...I've learned myself a lesson, a basic rule refresher,
That cow, the boat, and me can't hold our water under pressure!"

CHICKEN HOUSE ATTACK

The competition between beef and poultry has become a full time marketing theme, but rarely has it become as personal as "The Whitefield Chicken House Attack", aka "The Battle of the Bramer and the Broiler."

It was a hot summer afternoon in Haskell County, Oklahoma. The foggers and cooling fans were going full blast in Jim's twin 500 foot long chicken houses. "A wet chicken won't die" is the motto of polloqueros down south.

Sniffin' around the ten foot tall screen door at the south end of a chicken house was one of Jim's 700 pound black bramer-cross steers. Nibblin' on the rice hulls and litter, he pushed through the door and it slapped shut behind him.

"Blackie" froze for an instant. He found himself in this high, long metal building with more suspended, humping, fizzing, spritzing, undulating, augering, grinding, whirring water pipes, feed lines, sprinkler heads, fans, braces, cables, hoses and racket than the engine rooms of the Monitor and the Merrimac... not to mention the combined uproar of 25,000 startled chickens!

Blackie panicked, bore to the right and headed down the east wall leaping, smashing and obliterating the watering and cooling system that hung below the three foot level. Racing for the big door on the north end he careened along, bending the galvanized automated 500 foot long feedline into a mangled horseshoe. Jim, astride his four wheeler had seen the steer enter. He was racing alongside the building watching the mayhem through the 500 foot long chickenwire covered side window.

He screeched to a stop at the north door to open it and let Blackie escape...bad plan. Blackie saw him, turned back and tried to jump out the side window. The long span of chicken wire allowed him to actually exit the building but sprang him back like a trampoline into the pipes and feeders on the west side. Down the wall he went, demolishing everything in his path until he stopped midbarn to consider.

Jim four-wheeled it back to the south side door, propped it open and strode into the melee. Blackie pawed the ground. Feathers fluttered and litter flew. He charged. Jim, thinking quickly, reached down and armedhimself with two stomped flat chicken carcasses. Grasping their feet, he wielded them like a sword and a mace. Much noise ensued as hair and feathers flew but Jim prevailed and Blackie hightailed into a brush pile a hundred feet away.

Jim looked over his shoulder back into the Titanic. 24,998 chickens were pecking through the wreckage as if nothing had happened. He looked back to the brush pile. Blackie glared, shook his head and snorted fluff.

He looked like a busted pillowcase. And though he never came near the chicken house again, Jim said he could track him in the woods for days. He'd swallowed so many feathers his cow pies looked like decorations in the grass. Like big doilies on the back of grandma's lime green sofa.

CRIPPLE CREEK CALVIN & THE SNAKEY MARE

Calvin said he wasn't that good at getting' hurt. Of course, some would say he didn't have to try that hard. He's still ridin' bronky horses even though Homeland Security has him listed in the same category as Hurricane Katrina and a ten car pile up at the Indy 500.

Some would have thought he should have waited more than two months after knee surgery to try out the snakey mare. At least he started in the round corral. Some would say that naming his North Carolina ranch the Cripple Creek Livestock Company became a self-fulfilling prophecy. It explained his perpetual lameness.

The snakey mare was eight years old. Calvin knew her well. In anticipation he had asked the doctor to leave him some medial movement in his knee so he wouldn't always be jabbin' his horse with a spur. Good thinkin'.

He had made several circles inside the round pen when his grandson came out to watch. "Hi, Pawpaw!" Calvin stopped the mare in front of the boy. 'My bloodline,' thought Calvin. 'He'll be out here someday and I'll be leanin' on the fence.' "Make him wun, Pawpaw!"

"Naw, I..." He started to say as he shifted in the saddle to pat the boy on the back. Sensing his vulnerability, the mare bogged her head and commenced to bucking! She'd been savin' up and had plenty. Calvin never really got in rhythm with her. The grandson was heard to remark afterwards that Pawpaw looked like a slinky goin' down the stairs.

It had been a long time since Calvin had heard a bronc bawl like that. It's an eerie sound; a cross between an elk bugle and a lion's roar with a twang of tortured mule in there somewhere. She crashed to her knees, pitching Calvin forward over her neck. Then she reared back and rose up. Calvin would have mercifully fallen off except that his belt hooked over the saddlehorn! Some would say the next few seconds were reminiscent of a frenzied mating ritual involving a sea otter and a fire hose.

Calvin, in the re-telling of his final descent, remarked of a Zen-like experience where everything became slow motion. He flashed back on the memory of his friend Monica, a barrel racer. She, too, had gotten out over the top of her horse on the last barrel and hooked the front of her bra over the saddle horn. Calvin remembered thinking that, surely those puny hooks would break, not thinking it through that Monica was a full figured woman and had industrial strength hardware six inches wide across her back. She crossed the finish line lying on the horse like a surfboard.

The memory of Monica faded...

Calvin's meteor-like impact was slowed only by the fact that he tangled an arm in the coils of his rope on the way down which flipped him over, allowing him to land feet first...on his bad knee. He did the splits, injuring a groin muscle. The grandson clapped.

Some would say it was the end of a perfect cowboy day.

THE DOGS' COLUMN

NOTE: On occasion Baxter's dogs take over his column. Yes, they can type. 60 words a minute, give or take a minute, and use the spell checker.

By the way of introduction, let me say that I, Pancho Villa de Perro Valiente, am the new head of Ranch Security at the Black Rancho on Red Chile Road. I come from a long line of Australian Shepherd cowdogs and I am assisted by Hattie, hoof eater and Blue Heeler cross. You may be under the illusion that B. Black, cowboy poet, is an expert at ranching, an accomplished veterinarian and an equestrian authority. It is only true in the sense that the Montreal Expos claim to be a professional baseball team and that Cuba is considered a super power.

I admit Hattie and I like it when he shoes the horses. Lots of good nibblin's. Normally you wouldn't associate so much blood with farriery but 'cut to the quick' Black likes to get his money's worth. He only shoes his horses, not other peoples'. It is a practical decision, most people can't afford to have 'em lame that long.

We go with him to check the cows...15 head in two sections. You'd think after four years of checkin' the same arroyos and mesquite thickets he'd know where to look. No way, he wakes up in a new world every day. It's easier to follow the migration path of the bovine lungworm than to stay with him on a circle. And since he can't tell the cows apart he counts the same one three or four times. Management material, he ain't.

He and Francisco went to Gerald's brandin' last month, wouldn't let us go, the rat bag. Francisco told us later Gerald let Blacko drag calves to the fire. I said, sarcastically, "you mean 'calf' to the fire." Francisco said, "No, calves. He caught two, at the same time. One around the neck and the other around the front foot." Not bad for an hour's work.

One of the highlights of bein' Bumbling Black's dogs is the leftovers; quail innards, calf testicles, hoof trimmings, lizard tails, snake heads, cow horns, goldfish (from his tank maintenance program), and molasses from the tub feeder. As to his veterinary skills, I am thankful that he takes me and Hattie to Dr. Leverance. Hattie got snakebit again and I ate a box of D-Con... I know, but I just can't resist. She's saved us both more than once. Dr. "Ha Ha" Black did treat Chaco, his left-handed rope horse. He mostly did nuthin' so Chaco got well in spite of him.

It's not a bad life out here in rough country. We spend alot of quality time keepin' the birds off the bird feeder, barkin' at the coyotes and javelina or just trackin' ol' Bax around the place. Talk about a migrating lungworm, he's got unfinished projects scattered from the water trap to the sand pile. Never gets anything finished. Right now he's replanting some Bougainvillea in front of his shop. Poor fool. Oh, well. It'll only take me five minutes to dig'em up again.

That's it for now. Vaya con huesos,

Pancho Villa and Hattie
At the Black Ranch down on the border

COWBOY VOCABULARY MISCONCEPTIONS

My stories have an agricultural-cowboy slant. However, I am aware that urban people (Gentiles, I call them) may read this book as well. So when I lapse into my "cowboy vocabulary" I appreciate that some of my meanings could be unclear. Listed are some common misconceptions:

Statement: "My whole flock has keds."
Misinterpretation: Sheep are now endorsing tennis shoes.

Statement: "I'm looking to buy some replacement heifers but I want only polled cattle."
Misinterpretation: His cows are being interviewed by George Gallup.

Statement: "I'm going to a gaited horse show."
Misinterpretation: A horse performance being held in an exclusive residential area.

Statement: "I work in a hog confinement facility."
Misinterpretation: She teaches classes at the campus jail at University of Arkansas.

Statement: "I prefer the Tarentaise over the Piedmontese."
Misinterpretation: He is picky about cheese.

Statement: "They've had a lot of blowouts at the turkey farm this year."
Misinterpretation: Sounds like they better change tire dealers.

Statement: "This mule is just a little owly."
Misinterpretation: His ears stick up? He's wise beyond his specie limitation? No, wait, he looks like Benjamin Franklin or Wilford Brimley?

Statement: "Do you know where I could get a bosal, romal and some tapaderas?"
Misinterpretation: I'd suggest someplace that served Mexican food.

Statement: "I heard that Speed Williams and Rich Skelton got one down in five flat."
Misinterpretation: Must be a couple of quick anesthesiologists.

Statement: "I heard Texas has now gotten Brucellosis free."
Misinterpretation: I assume Bruce, who is of Greek origin, finally got a good lawyer.

Statement: "The Beef Check Off has gone up to a dollar."
Misinterpretation: Not a bad price for a Russian sandwich. I know the Veal Solginetzen and the Chicken Zhavago are twice that much.

Statement: "You don't have to be a genius to see that the team pulls to the left."
Misinterpretation: Whoever they are were not satisfied with the election results.

Statement: "I believe that Debouillet has blue bag."
Misinterpretation: She's taken to wearing French fashion accessories.

Statement: "That horse won't break out of a canter."
Misinterpretation: Then that's what I'd keep him in. Beats tyin' him to a post.

Statement: "She's wormed, fresh offa wheat grass and showin' a little ear."
Misinterpretation: A modest stripper on an organic diet has swallowed her chewing tobacco.

Statement: "You can stick a fork in me."
Correct interpretation: He's done.

WANDA AND THE WILD HEIFER

It was a cold starry night somewhere in West River, Dakotaland. Calving had been under way a couple weeks. Ed and Wanda were already into the heifer checking routine.

On this particular night Wanda had taken the middle-of-the-night duty. Ed had stayed up late trying to fix a water leak in the barn. Water pipes are buried deep up north. Ed had dug a hole big enough to bury a small mule. Grunt work – frozen ground, mud under the permafrost. He located the break, shut off the main line and called it quits for the night.

After Wanda reheated supper for him, he hit the hay. It was midnight and he fell asleep, exhausted. Wanda set her alarm for 2:30 am. She'd make the deep in the night heifer check and let Ed rest. Ranch wives are the unsung work force in the glamorous panorama of the romantic life of the cowboy.

Imagine, if you will, instead of billboards depicting the handsome, macho Marlboro Man, you see a full color spread of a red-faced woman with steamed up glasses wearing lumpy, well-used canvas coveralls, her nighty wadded up around her waist, poking out above the zipper, maybe a torn down jacket with dehorning blood on the sleeve, hair sticking out underneath a ratty wool stocking cap, mismatching gloves and muddy slip-on rubberized moon boots that look more like deer liver than clothing.

The alarm woke Wanda. She bundled up and stomped out to the barn. She moved one nervous heifer from the calving lot into the barn. The heifer did not like the move and got on the fight. Wanda tried to bluff. It didn't work. The heifer charged! Wanda scrambled over the portable panels that comprised the sides of the pen and fell...right into the hole Ed had dug earlier. The heifer tried to jump the panels after her but succeeded only in knocking it over – right on top of the hole, trapping Wanda underneath.

Then, just when you were thinking, 'poor Wanda,' the heifer landed feet first on top of the panel, driving all four legs down through the bars.

Wanda lay flat on her back as four bovine cloven hooves paddled furiously 12 inches above her frayed and frigid evening wear. It was like the fish-eye view of swimming cows. Four hours later Ed woke up, shaved, made the coffee, and came out to the barn looking for the love of his life.

CONTEST OF WILLS

Loading a cow is a contest of wills, usually between a 4-legged beast with a thick skull and a stubborn streak and a 2-legged beast with a thick skull and a stubborn streak.

Shawn and Rick had sorted off the ignorant pig (not a literal biological description, but rather a personality classification) into the loading pen. Both ahorseback, they tried to push her into the loading alley. She'd circle, turn back, charge the horses, blow snot, run into the fence and try to scale the wall. Anything but load.

The wall, or fence, as it were, was hard to scale. It consisted of railroad ties set five inches apart, stockade style, and standing six feet tall. There was no danger of her escaping.

Shawn, decision maker of the two, grew frustrated, as in "I'll load that no good, snake eatin', no loadin', head down, sorry excuse for a tail draggin' salt licker...Rick; git off yer horse!"

They both dismounted. Following instructions, Rick applied the 'Hulk Hogan tail twist' to the thousand pound, on-the-fight, polled, cactus eating, bag of buzzard bait (again, a personality classification). Shawn guided her with a handy piece of humane cow director, shaped like a 2 x 4.

They got her within 2 feet of the alley neck when she whirled, did a 180 and looked Rick in the eye. Rick turned and ran. He maintained a 12 inch lead as they raced across the loading pen. He was looking over his shoulder when he ran out of pen.

Like Roadrunner into the cliff, he hit the wall a full second before she licked the stamp and stuck him to it! (Author's note: one does not slide down the face of a creosote railroad tie as smoothly as down a tiled wall. Tar and splinters give it the Velcro effect.) Meanwhile the cow turned back into the pen like a man-eating shark in the shallow end of the pool. She pawed the ground and charged Shawn!

Engaging his cowboy mentality, he drew back the board in baseball bat fashion, unfortunately she threw a fast ball. He misjudged, swung late, the crack Rick heard was not the bat, but a rib. She caught him full frontal.

He was doubled over her head, arms around her neck, clinging desperately to avoid getting pulled down under the trampling feet as she plowed across the dirt.

Alas, he went down in front of the locomotive legs and she trampled over him! He rolled - then unrolled - flat out, belly to the sun. From their crumpled viewpoint Rick and Shawn watched this fine Brangus cow scan the battlefield, turn, and walk down the alley up into the trailer.

"There," said Shawn, scratching his thick skull and rubbing his stubborn streak, "Just right."

KELLEY AND THE SUPER COWBOY

"You could use a little help," the boss told Kelley one morning at the horse barn. "I know yer doin' a good job but sometimes an extra hand can make it easier. Besides, the kid needs the work, although I'm told he's a super cowboy, he's in a slump."

'The kid', turned out to be a down-on-his-luck bronc rider on whom the boss had taken pity. His bad luck hadn't affected his super cowboy confidence, though. "I kin ride anything with hair and, if I may say, I'm a good hand with a rope...if you've got an extry I could borrow," said the kid upon meeting Kelley the first time.

That next day Kelley rigged the kid up with one of the boss's saddles, a head stall and, an extra rope. The only gear the kid had with him was a hack rein, rodeo chaps and a bronc saddle, none of which had much value for ranch work.

They rode out into the foggy coastal California morning to gather a bull and a cow-calf pair. At first sight of the cowboys, the bull ran for cover. They tried to turn him back to no avail. "Rope him," said Kelley. The super cowboy missed. Kelley managed to catch a head and a front leg. The kid missed a couple more till Kelley finally told him to get behind and push.

Half an hour later they came back for the pair, a big, high horned rangy lookin' yellow cow that easily weighed 1,400 pounds, and her 2-month old calf. With surprising ease they got them all the way across the verdant hillside pasture to the gate. Then suddenly the cow whirled, dived between them and headed back to the oak trees. Kelley swung a quick loop and snagged the calf. He was off his horse and on the calf quicker than a tarantula wasp, and tied him down. He looked around to ask the kid's help dragging the bawling calf through the gate. Then all they would have to do was wait for mama cow to come back and claim her baby.

But the kid had taken it upon himself to catch the cow. Kelley watched as he raced across the damp pasture accompanied by his two border collies in pursuit of the hightailin' cow. Kelley noticed the kid was a fearless rider. The cow slipped on the wet ground and went down momentarily. The kid rode by at a high lope, dropped his loop over the cow's head and tried to swing his horse around. Not in time. The cow rose, the dally missed, the horse stumbled. It was a great wreck. A twinge of admiration crossed Kelley's mind as he saw the kid jerked from the saddle, both hands on the rope, and go sailing after the cow.

Kelly watched unbelieving as the cow thundered across the slick grass draggin' the super cowboy like a tuna tied behind a speedboat. They were headed right for the calf. Completing the scene came the two super cow dogs in the rear, drivin' the horse, fenders flappin', tail ringin' and reins flyin' in the wake of the cow and her tenacious passenger.

"How's the kid workin' out?" the boss asked Kelley later.

"Fine. Just fine." answered Kelley, with the smile of a man who had found another source of great cowboy memories for future exaggeration and retelling.

IMMORTAL BRANDING

I got bucked off the other day, alas it was nothing new.
I's settin' on a borrowed horse, the rope was old, the bruise is blue.

Thank goodness everyone was there, they never miss a branding.
The geezers come to just help out but nothing too demanding.

They mostly come to catch first hand some wreck or temper riling.
I guess I really made their day, I saw they all were smiling.

I'd double hocked a heifer calf and started for the flankers
But they were backed up, left no time to toss out any anchors.

My dally slipped, she took the slack and started to skidaddle.
The rope flipped up across my waist and slicked me off the saddle

Just like I'd rode beneath a tree or hit a power line.
I lit and rolled and bounced back up like everything was fine.

The geezers gathered round and asked "Hurt?" "Nope," I lied, "It doesn't."
They seemed so disappointed. Was like they were hurt I wasn't.

But they'd make do. Ya see, the seed of the story was planted,
For weeks my rep would be discussed with n'er a mercy granted.

Yes, history was set on course, no doubt to be rewritten
Each time a geezer told the tale.   In truth it's only fittin'

'Cause that's how Pecos Bill was born and Wyatt Earp and others
Like Pancho Villa, Sitting Bull, Will Pickett and his brothers.

Charles Goodnight, Casey Tibbs, we bid vaya con Dios,
All legends in our cowboy world we honor now as heroes.

So my mishap could be the start of my own legacy
That years from now will see great marble statues carved of me.

My picture framed will hang on walls, my likeness carved in leather,
My name will be a household word wherever cowboys gather.

But in the meantime I must bear the taunts and jibes that linger
Of when I bucked off some kid's horse and broke my little finger.

CALVING MISDIAGNOSIS

It is the bad dream of the rancher's wife during calving season. Not as bad as a blizzard or machinery wreck but worse than having to go to Kingfisher for parts.

Hubby's been gone overnight so Shirla saddles up to go check the new calves in the calving lot. It's cold enough to freeze the muddy spots but it's a sunny morning. She spots a heifer on her side, her abdomen is tight and she's straining. Dismounting, Shirla approaches the beast for a closer look. No feet sticking out.

A call on her cell phone to father-in-law down the road proves fruitless, no one answers. So back to the house she rides to get her teenage daughter.

"I'm gonna need yer help," Mom says.

"Ma-Um," whines the daughter in two syllables, "I've just done my hair, I've got on my school clothes!"

"Pull on yer coveralls, grab some boots, I can't do it alone!"

Ten minutes later the two of them return to the pen. Shirla is carrying a length of rope and some O.B. chains. The cow is in even more trouble, breathing in gasps, grossly distended abdomen, yet still no sign of the calf.

They put a loop around the cow's hind legs. Shirla instructs her daughter, "I'll hold the rope, you stick your hand in there and find the calf...your hands are smaller!"

"No way!" said daughter in an exaggerated tone, as if she'd been asked to jump in a barrel of soft-boiled eggs or wear something decent!

"I've just done my nails!"

"There's no time to lose!" said Shirla, handing the rope to her daughter. Shirla got her arm inside the cow past her wrist and could feel nothing.

"Are you sure you're in the right hole?" asked the daughter.

"Of course!" she said, shoving on in up to the elbow.

The cow was pushing back, grunting and struggling to get upright.

"Pull on that rope!" Shirla shouted and forced her arm in up to the shoulder.

"It's so tight," she said, "but I still can't find the calf!"

"That might be him up there by her head," said a voice she recognized as her father-in-law's.

"What?" asked Shirla, looking up to see a calf curled like a cat contentedly sleeping ten feet away. She looked down at her arm and at the cow, who for one brief moment raised her head high enough to look back at her torturer.

"Well, " she stammered, "what's the matter with . . ."

"Bloat," he answered, "I'll go get the hose."

THE CEMENT POUR

"Have you seen Mauna Loa?" I asked Will.

"No," he replied, as a foot high wall of concrete began covering his boot toes.

"It's a volcano in Hawaii," I explained.

The cement truck driver added to our education by pointing out that 5 yards of concrete weighs 20,000 pounds. It's not that we were complete novices around cement, sand and gravel. We have poured footings, built rock walls, patched old water tanks, shoveled out feed bunks and irrigation ditches, and driven over lots of concrete cattle guards. But alas, in retrospect we put too much faith in plywood and drywall screws.

We built a form. It looked good, but then again I live in a land where the illusion of a fence is considered as good as five strands of bob wire and a post every eight feet. We stack things against rusty wire and make extensive use of stays fashioned from willow branches, mesquite limbs, string, BBQ grills, car parts, hoe handles, cardboard, pillowcases and coyote hides.

The form was to be for a free standing stem wall, 4' x 2' x 16', thus 4.74 cu. yards. It was plumbed, braced and photographed for the archives. 7 a.m. on the dot the giant concrete truck rumbled in. The driver backed up to the spot and swung his long chute out over the open top of our form. It looked like the dull oviposter on a gargantuan wasp squatting over a tarantula's hole.

In retrospect, I realize the driver had probably seen "cowboy projects" before and anticipated excitement. "Are you ready?" he asked gleefully. "Let'er rip!" I said like a man in front of a firing squad.

Standing next to a cement mixer truck as tons of gravelly concrete roll down the chute can rattle your brain. As the cement reached the 2' level, the sides of the form began to bulge. Will asked, "Do you have any cardboard?" An interesting question, I remembered thinking. Something General Custer might have asked as the Indians closed in on him.

We tried to stem the bulge by driving stakes in the ground but the gray mass simply wedged its shoulder under the form and lifted it off the ground!

"STOP!" The churning mixer stopped. Another 900 lbs of concrete clattered into the form. A tide of lava surged from underneath and rolled the length of 2 shovel handles before it sludged to a stop at Will's feet.

"Mauna Loa?" he repeated, "never seen it."

"Yeah," I said, "But now you don't have to . . ."

PENNSYLVANIA SHEEP DOCTOR

A man with bandaged hands and welts on his face limped painfully into the doctor's exam room. A nurse held out two latex gloves and said,

"This is probably going to hurt."

"Yeeow!" said the doctor.

Dr. Dave, gentle doctor, community leader and backyard sheep person, winced as the tight gloves snapped on his excoriated hands. He told the story for the 10th time that morning. "You see, I shear my own sheep."

It gives him a feeling of completeness and self-reliance to be up to the task of being a good shepherd. Dr. Dave has a little farm in the wooded rolling hills of eastern Pennsylvania. However it immediately places him in that 1% of sheep owners who shear their own sheep, horse owners who shoe their own horses and politicians without lawyers.

He hadn't exactly planned to begin shearing that afternoon but he'd put it off long enough. After scattering some feed, he took his rope and bare-handed dropped it on the head of his big Polypay ram. It was at that moment that his cowboy mentality kicked in and blindfolded his good judgment. A big ewe was also busily attacking the grain, so...he quickly tied a loop in the other end of the rope and dropped it over her head. (Who says an education is protection against a brain meltdown?) He placed himself midrope and began to lead the two sheep barnward.

He later estimated he was in the lead for less than 5 seconds. Off they raced across the green pasture dragging his body alternately prone, belly up, feet first, headfirst, water-skiing, swan diving, jack knifing, plow-ing, skimming and screaming across the slick grass. To his credit he clung like a stuffed goat bladder tied between two galloping Mongolian ponies.

The ewe took the lead and shot through the gate. Dr. Dave flew after her, noticing for a split second the decorative bluebird house he had placed atop the gate post. Alas, it had never attracted any bluebirds, but there was something...?

The ram, running a close third, hit the birdhouse head-on arous-ing its occupants...oh, yes...a nest of hornets. They bore down on the only bare-skinned member of the thundering trio and showed their displea-sure.

Dave only managed to stop the sheep by tangling himself in the rope and getting wedged crossways under an antique hay rake. As he lay sideways against the wheel rim contemplating his blistered palms, swell-ing face and sore bones, he heard his wife call from the back door, "Honey, need any help?"

BOB BLACK '06

61

BUFFALO TRADING

The lure to own something of historical significance is strong. Benjamin Franklin's signature, an arrowhead, Dale Evan's Chapstick. This connection to tradition is part of the popularity of raising buffalo, I think. However, putting bison on display on your farm is more 'complicated' than parking an antique tractor in your shed.

Kenny was having a clearance sale. He had four buffalo cows and one bull up for sale. A country gentleman with 20 acres called and a deal was made. The gentleman assured Kenny he knew what he was doing. His wife and he already had two llamas and an emu, and he had seen *Dances With Wolves*.

He showed up at Kenny's place in a brand new Chevy 3/4 ton pickup and a 20' stock trailer that didn't have a scratch or speck of manure on it. Kenny's own buffalo hauling trailer looked more like an armored car or the bed of a dump truck. He looked at the 3/4-inch pipe and tin foil sides of the gentlemen's rig and decided to keep his mouth shut. It took the gentleman 30 minutes and 40 acres to get backed up to the loading chute. He walked back wearing his brand new black cowboy hat, boots, and a buffalo head bolo tie carrying a bullwhip.

"What do I do?" he asked.

"Sit in the pickup till I get 'em loaded," said Kenny

The cows complied but the bull was being difficult. Finally Kenny got him up to where he was sniffing the trailer floor when the gentleman poked his head around the corner, spooking the bull and causing Kenny to dive for cover!

After re-instructing the gentleman to stay in the truck, Kenny snapped a long lead rope to a chain that hung from a ring in the bull's nose. He then ran the lead rope around a pipe in the trailer, took a dally on a corral post and worked the bull back up the chute right to the trailer again.

Once again, in a effort to help, the gentleman peered around the corner, scaring the bull who pulled back so hard the snap broke! The lead rope whipped around, the broken snap cracked across the gentleman and broke his arm!

"What do I do?" cried the gentleman.

"Stay in the truck!"

The third time was the charm; the bull loaded with a little help from a plastic bag and a fence stay. He circled and banged inside the new trailer while the gentleman counted out the cash with his good arm. Suddenly the bull charged the tailgate, got a horn under one horizontal bar and ripped 3 of them loose! The welds popped like snaps on a shirt! He stuck his head out.

"What do I do!" hollered the gentleman from the cab.

"They're not mine," said Kenny "but I believe 'bout every couple minutes I'd slam on the brakes to keep him from makin' the hole bigger."

Kenny watched as the truck and trailer headed down his driveway with the buffalo stickin' out like a trophy on the den wall. Then he heard the screech of brakes and saw the buffalo disappear!

Tradition don't come easy.

AVIAN FLU FOBIA

During the worldwide epidemic of Avian Flu, it was a frequent topic of television, radio and magazine headlines. It is well-known that over-saturation of frightening headlines can result in public apathy but in this case it heightened the awareness of one very supersensitive person.

Susu was a new mother. A career woman with company health insurance and a loving husband. She read the books, took the lessons, watched the video and bore a beautiful baby boy named Leopold. Leopold lived his first 18 months as if he were Prince Charles' firstborn. Cooed over, mentally stimulated, abundantly loved, and protected. Protected? Did I say protected? With every all-natural, Dr. Suess- approved, boneless, childproof, soft and fluffy, non-allergenic, paranoid restriction, followed to the letter.

Aunt Bea invited Susu and Leopold on a trip to the zoo. "He won't have any contact with the animals will he?" asked Susu. "I've read about the threat of Foot and Mouth Disease, Rabies, Tuberculosis, Brucellosis and Mad Cow Disease!" Aunt Bea explained that the animals were all in cages and they wouldn't actually get close to the inmates. "Yes, but monkeys throw their droppings, ya know, and what if an elephant sneezed! He could catch elephantiasis!" With a stroller packed full of tin foil, raincoats, an umbrella and blue plastic tarp they entered the zoo. Leopold was wrapped in a hooded pullover. He looked like a tree frog in a tube sock.

The zoo pathway was lined with trees, full of birds; squawking, cackling, whistling, hooting, shrieking, chirping birds. "Oh no!" said Susu, clutching little Leopold, "What about Avian Flu!" Aunt Bea reassured Susu that she was worrying too much. After they had moved from under the canopy of trees, away from the ornithene cacophony, she convinced Susu to uncover Leopold's little head.

Standing in front of the rhino cage under a sparkling sky Susu finally relaxed and stepped back to take a snapshot of Aunt Bea holding Leopold. Bea lifted Leopold high up in the air as if to show him his kingdom. Streaking from behind an errant cloud like a dive-bomber, a lone feathered strafer crossed above the pleasant family outing and lightened his load. Just as the camera snapped, the laser guided projectile splatted noisily square on top of Leopold's baby-haired noggin!

The photo on close-up showed a startled Aunt Bea, a rhino horn and a smiling baby Leopold with what looked like a fried egg on his head.

Handiwipes - $2.39/box...photo – priceless!

OLD WAYS DIE HARD

The old ways die hard. Even after Gary converted his western Nebraska cow operation to four-wheelers, Ambro still thought of the mechanical monster as his horse.

"I broke the horse," Ambrosia said in his melodious Spanish accent. Gary had found him waiting at the little office when he came to work at 6:30 am. Ambro had always said 'I don't want the sun to get too heavy on me', so he started early.

"You broke the horse?" asked Gary, ready for anything. "What do you mean?"

According to Ambro, he had been out sorting cow-calf pairs that morning. One big calf kept ducking under the 3-strand barbwire fence. Frustrated, Ambro took his 'horse' through the wire gate to get the calf back. He had been a bueno vaquero in his youth and prided himself on his roping. He tied hard and fast to the mechanical saddlehorn and took up the chase.

The handlebar clutch, throttle and brake 'reins' made swinging his loop and carrying his coils a little unwieldy. The calf was quick and led Ambro around the flat and through the swales like dry leaves being chased by a lawnmower.

In the clattering banging commotion Ambro dropped a coil, maybe two, around a front tire which promptly tightened against the knot tied to the handlebar saddlehorn which jerked the 'horse' to a stop.

Ambro dismounted, got enough slack in the line to peel the rope off the wheel horse's foot. It took off...by itself! Being still in 3rd high, the chase gear, it began making circles around the vaquero who held tight to the other end of the rope like a lunge line. All he needed was a whip to complete the training picture.

"I tink," he had explained to Gary, "I should let go...what could happen?" He did, his 'horse' disappeared over a hump in the direction of the cows, going home like all good horses do.

Ambro chased it but it could run faster. He topped the rise and surveyed the scene below. "I don't know Boss, but it hit the fence, turn sideways under the wire, and run along below. It was liftin' up the wire and tearin' out the T-posts till it hit the wooden railroad tie. It was bouncing up and down on its hind legs like Trigger tryin' to jump it. I went up to him real easy and said 'whoa' and switch the key. But it was too late...my horse was broke."

Gary was pounding his desk and snorting like a Percheron. Tears were streaming down his face. He was gasping.

Ambro was confused. In his polite old country way, he said, "I wanted to laugh, too, but . . . my breath got away and I had to catch it first."

OUT THERE

I do commentary on National Public Radio headquartered in Washington D.C. It is heavily urban in listenership. Some have questioned why NPR includes my commentaries. So have I. When I asked, the producer said, "Because you're the only one we know...from out there."

Out there. Where exactly is...out there? When I look south from my veranda I can see as far back in time as Coronado, who rode up the river horseback and came within five miles of my house. That was in 1535, three hundred years before those johnny-come-lately's Lewis and Clark caught a ride with the locals to Ft. Pierre.

When I look toward the north on a crystal clear night I can see as far away as Polaris, axle of the Big Dipper. It shines directly down on the outposts of civilization. Omak, Sandpoint, Viking, Culbertson, Maple Creek, Elgin, Eagle Butte and Newcastle. Settlements as self-sufficient and self-reliant as a space station on the surface of the moon. Places where people and elm trees send down roots and look with pity at those who have to send out for pizza at ten til seven because they don't have their act together.

When I look to the sunrise I can see clear back to the palmetto and piney woods, Cumberland Gaps and cornfields. Where many of the gringo ancestors walked and rode and intermarried and populated the Llano Estacado, the arid plains, the holes in the walls and the ends of the roads. Like the boll weevil, lookin' for a home.

When I look to the setting sun I can hear the jingle of the bit chains, the swish of the lariat, the beat of the drum, and war cry of the natives and Spaniards who named the places we live; Maricopa, Kaibab, Santa Rosa, Tonapah, Tillamook, Durango and Winnemucca, and still live there.

When I look down I can see the paw print of a mountain lion in a sandy wash, the outline of a steel shoe that I nailed to my horse's foot, a black porous rock that was belched up from earth's inferno before people walked here. And the track of my son who passed this way this morning out to do the chores.

And when I look up I can hear the silence, the rustle of things jostling for position in space. The cry of the coyote and the heavenly admonition to use the place responsibly, to appreciate its harsh beauty and to pick up the trash.

Out there. A vast part of this country from the Sierras to the backwoods, north and south as far as you can point, where the tracks are further apart and you can see the stars at night.

Out there. No better, no worse, just a little leaner and closer to the bone.

When the NPR producer had said, "Because you're the only one from out there," I wondered if he meant geographically or philosophically?

I'm still not sure.

HEY COWGIRL, NEED A RIDE?

You can talk about the glamour
and the love of rodeo
The challenge and the heartbreak
of the dally and the throw
Of the guts and luck and glory,
the leather and the sweat
The gristle and the power
of the bull that ain't rode yet

And the get up-in-the-morning
and the miles-down-the-road
And the bronc that stands awaitin'
and the rope that ain't been throwed
The vision of the buckle
worn by superhuman champs
And paid for in contusions,
broken bones, in aches and cramps

And mothers in the bleachers
and spouses back at home
Who keep the home fires burning
while their darlin' loved ones roam
The siren's call of rodeo
that beckons one last ride
The gambler's itch, the mountain top,
the pinnacle, the pride

The reason they give all they have
is measured in a score
A crowd, a millisecond,
flag and timer, judge and roar
But for some the lure is simpler,
the attraction that still pulls
Like me...just gettin' girls
was the reason I rode bulls!

THE AUCTION BARN MIRACLE!

If ya hang around a sale barn long enough you are bound to see some strange, some would say supernatural happenings. Like a cattle buyer actually bidding a penny over the market, or a waiter in a tuxedo at the sale barn café, or what happened to Chato and the Indian cow.

Sonny said when the truck arrived from the reservation a lot of the cows were thin but the last one required gentle assistance to unload. She was doing poorly, a common lookin' whiteface cow with a wide muzzle, ringed horns, bony hips and a long tail. A T-11 brand as well as several hieroglyphic brands decorated her hide.

Chato came in to report that the cow in question was now, and as he put it, 'has been dead all day long!" Sonny sent two cowboys to the pen. Sure 'nuf she was still dead. They hooked onto her hind legs with ropes, pulled her from the tight stockyard pen, down three alleys and out to the road.

Chato picked her limp body up with the front-end loader. Sonny checked her ID's and watched as her head hung over the bucket draining digestive fluids. She was lowered gently in the dump truck and laid to wait for the final trip.

Since it was noon, Sonny suggested Chato eat his lunch and deliver the dead beast afterwards. Sonny did the paperwork and went on to the next crisis. Then, unexpectedly he heard what sounded like the Navy's crack acrobatic team of Blue Angels roaring over the sale yard at the speed of jet fuel! Thinking they would be strafed, he clutched his chest then realized to his relief it was only the old dump truck, pedal to metal, black smoke billowing and the iron bed rattling like chains on the gates of hell!

Sonny ran outside to see Chato, brakes locked, sliding through the gravel in a cloud of dust! Chato stopped, crashed out of the door and turned back to look. The crazy-eyed cow was looking down at Chato with a malevolent glare. With the bright sunlight at her back, her eyes glistened out of a silhouetted black head with horns. "¡Es un diablo!" yelled Chato as he staggered away.

While Chato was catching his breath and genuflecting, the boys drove the dump truck into a pen. Two of them held the tailgate up as the bed was tilted. The resurrected cow slid, upright, all four feet splayed out like a novice on the bunny hill. She hit the ground running, on the fight and put 'em all over the fence.

The following week she went through the sale as unnoticed as Clark Kent. Sonny thought it was best to leave sleeping cows lie.

THE PETTING ZOO

In the next county over they are experiencing the incursion of urban development. In other words, business is booming! Sprawl, malls, concrete, traffic, crime, and the herd mentality reigns.

Country people still populate the fringes and the county fair is functioning and vibrant, despite the annual attacks of people who dislike it. Some of these people are well meaning, some have an agenda, but it is fair to say, most have no real experience or connection to livestock.

I called a man who had written a particularly scathing letter to the editor. We had a civil discussion. He was a well-spoken, sensitive man and made two points; that the petting zoo is inhumane and it was heart wrenching when a little girl had to sell her show hog. I agreed with both. I have, on occasion, manned the petting zoo myself and felt inhumanely treated. Then again, I've never been good at daycare or helping with little kids at school. I just can't yell that long.

He, of course, thought the little lambs, pigs, burros, puppies, kittens, calves and ducklings were being tortured. All manner of ruly and unruly urban children were chasing, petting, touching, carrying, kissing and hugging the cuddly critters. Their laughing and childish joy was no doubt frightening to the little animals.

But one of the jobs of the people on "petting zoo duty" is to prevent any harm, which we do well. The point of the whole project is to lend reality to animals that most urban kids know only as stuffed toys, animated talking cartoons, or reduced images on a TV screen. There is wonderment in their discovery, and we hope, a beginning of respect for the animal kingdom they could never get watching *The Animal Planet*.

Regarding the little girl's tears over the sale of her pig, we in the real world of livestock, know it first hand. It is part of our life. When my daughter was eleven, she was showing her dear urban aunt her rabbits. The aunt was holding a cute little bunny and asked my daughter what she does with them.

"When they reach five pounds we butcher them for the grocery store."

"How can you do that!" Auntie gasped!

And with the wisdom of a child she said, *"I don't make friends with them."*

But we do, now and then. Make friends, I mean. A loyal cow, a good dog, an orphan lamb, a bottle calf, a trustworthy horse. We devote time and care to them, and they respond. A bond is formed. But it is a relationship wherein we know the final outcome. We accept it as their lot in life. Knowing their fate may be the strongest factor in creating the respect we feel for them as individuals.

It would be nice to think at a petting zoo somewhere this summer, a new world will be opened for some little human. A feeling stirred in some 4-year-old heart. The wet nose of a calf, or the softness of a little chick, that could transcend Star Wars, Barney, Legos, Barbie and Pop Tarts, and restore in them our ancient connection to the real Earth.

Bring yer kids. We do.

COW DANCING

The pour-on instructions said, DANGER: Pay attention and get this
part right!
Use branding irons with much precaution. The fumes are inclined to
ignite.

"WHOA BACK, JACK! MY COW'S ON FIRE!"
"No kiddin'," Jack spoke through the flames.
"WELL DON'T JUST STAND THERE, PUT HER OUT! WE'VE GOT NO
TIME TO PLAY GAMES."

"WHATAYA DOIN' YA NINCOMPOOP!"
"It's a 2 x 4, whataya think."
"YOU CAN'T STOP A FIRE WITH A 2 x 4.
IT'LL NEVER WORK, TRY YOUR CHINKS!"

"Try yer own. I'm just the hired help."
"DO SOMETHIN'! SHE'LL GET OVERHEATED,"
"How's this, 'Dear Lord, please save this cow.
And...Dear Larry, expletive deleted."

This whole thing transpired in just seconds.
The fumes caught on fire with a whoosh.
It made a big pop like a snappin' sheet
and flared like a creosote bush.

But in that short time Jack and Larry
resembled the Keystone cops.
They splashed on a thermos of coffee,
a bottle of Peppermint Schnapps.

They climbed in the squeeze chute like monkeys
and danced on her back in the smoke
to stomp out the mini inferno.
They tried disco, the polka and folk.

They hefted up both of their cow dogs
to get 'em to lift up their leg
They captured a guinea in passing
to try and squeeze out an egg.

"YER HAT! USE YER HAT!" cried out Larry.
Jack raised a barbecued brow.
"Yer dumber than boiled gravel.
My hat's worth more than your cow!"

"You could call the famed Forest Service
on your cellular phone or your fax
And order a single smoke jumper
to parachute in with his axe."

"Or smother the flames with your slicker,
if you'd brought it, but, no, you refrained,
Knowing that she wouldn't need it
if it was pourin' down rain."

They argued like this for an hour.
This ruckus was soon overblown.
The arson inspector was summoned
though the cow had gone out on her own.

"It's a pure case of simple malfeasance.
"Just stupid," the inspector said.
"I'd arrest you for preheating jerky
but you ain't got a brain in your head!

"I could cite you as an accomplice,
inciting her carnal desire
By stimulating hot flashes
which added fuel to the fire.

"But the charge I'm writing you up for
is an old law, though not obsolete,
For cow dancing after she's fired up.
Or, at least, while she's still in heat."

DEFINITION OF A COWBOY

I've often been asked the question, usually by gentiles (urban people) what my definition of a cowboy is. I'm not sure what they expect my answer to be. Maybe someone who is strong, forthright and brave? Or a professional rodeo hand? Or a movie star idol like John Wayne?

Although those answers do cover facets of cowboydom, they miss the heart of the job description. My definition of a cowboy is *someone who can replace a uterine prolapse in a range cow in a three section pasture with nothing but a horse and a rope.*

Thinkin' that through you can see the breadth of the skills and experience required. There are many people who can ride a horse better than a regular cowhand. Many who can outrope him. Also others who are smoother or more qualified to replace a prolapse. But not many who can do it all . . . by themselves.

The first thing that defines a cowboy is that he is there, on the scene, on duty to herd, guard, watch, protect, serve and save the cow. Range cows are good size critters a long way from the vet clinic. Which means if she is in trouble the lone cowboy is often the difference between life and death for her. Whether she's stuck in a mud bog, mauled by a mountain lion, hung in a tree fork, shot by an arrow, afflicted with pneumonia, attacked by screw worms or prolapsed.

To help her, first she has to be restrained. Even though they are domesticated animals - they are not tame. So the cowboy must be able to approach her horseback, to capture her, then hold her so he can work on the ailment. This first part of the definition involves quite a bit. Say you rope her. What do you do then? There's no corrals, no squeeze chute, no cowboy assistant, tranqualizer gun, winch or net, so you neck her to a tree or trip her then sideline or cross-tie her with a piggin' string.

Part 2, putting in the prolapse. This is no small procedure even in the antiseptic surroundings of a veterinary clinic. It's still like stuffing a smoked ham down a sink drain. It's no easier on the banks of a cottonwood creek or on the shale hillside of a winter permit.

But whether it's a prolapse, a wire around the foot, or a sick calf, the Palo Duro Canyon, the Tonto Basin or the Alvord Desert, it's still cowboy, horse and rope. The basic essentials.

I've overheard people compare the abilities of trick ropers, bronc riders, horse trainers and veterinarians to those of the workin'-for-wages cowboy. Observing that he is not as accomplished at their individual skills as they are. They seem disappointed.

I remind these folks that he is not a professional cowboy. He just does it for a living.

HIGH-HORNED RED COW'S CALF

I have calved a lot of heifers in my life...thousands. All of us who have that type of experience know that after the sweat and strain, the slick and sticky, the hope and pull, the grunt and sigh, when the wet little creature plops on the ground, sometimes there is a moment that time stands still. A second, or two or five, we stare, our world suspended, waiting for a sign.

Then the new baby sniffs, or blinks, or sneezes, or wiggles an ear, and at that moment it feels as though a burden has been lifted from our shoulders. We did it. We did it again. Just regular common people like us, engaged in that age old profession of stockman, have participated in a miracle; life being passed from one generation to the next.

It is no small thing to be a part of and every time it happens, it renews us. The miracle never diminishes. As urbanization inexorably isolates people from the land, fewer and fewer humans are able to participate in this ancient experience. It is our loss, as a species.

Last year, after we had finished calving at my place, none of the cows had needed help, for which I was thankful. But each new little critter trailing after his mama or kickin up his heels made me smile.

Finally the high horned red cow calved. Baby was solid red like mama. I sat there the next day ahorseback and studied him for a few minutes. Long enough to figure out it was a bull calf and getting plenty to eat. Satisfied, I swung away and started back through the mesquite on a cow trail. I heard a mama bawlin and looked back to see that it was the high horned red cow. I swept the horizon for her calf, then looked down. There he was right behind my horse s hind leg trailin along with us. I stopped. The little calf bumped into my stirrup. He looked confused. He could hear his mama but something didn t smell right. I reached down and patted his head. He looked up at me, as if to say, What are you doin here?

About that time my dog stuck his nose to the baby s tail. He jumped like a deer, straight legged and trotted back toward his mama in his ungainly tryin out his new legs, kinda gait. It was pretty funny. The dog and I couldn t help but laugh.

Illustration by Julie Rice ©2006

TILT TABLE VS ROPING

Springtime.   Grass is greenin' up, wildflowers are blooming, longjohns are comin' off, and it's brandin' time! It is a festive occasion on lots of ranches. For years it has become a time for neighbors to get together and help one another.

The cows and calves have been gathered the day before. By daylight horses have been unloaded, everybody's saddled up and the calves are sorted from their mamas. In the corral propane burners and branding pots are set up, brands heating, vaccine guns loaded, ear tags laid out, and dad's knife is sharp enough to clean a hornfly's fingernails!

Idyllic...right?

Wait...technology has reared its sleek, rancher's helper-automated-finger mashing-clanging-banging head, in the form of a tilt table calf squeeze chute!

So nowadays when your neighbor invites you to come help him brand his calves you mumble around. You're feeling him out as to whether he's still roping them and dragging them to the fire *or* pushing them through a long narrow alley, catching them in a calf chute and immobilizing the wiggling beasts. Sure, you appreciate that it's easier on the calves, the help, the horses, that it takes less time and labor, even less space than the traditional way, but it's so...mechanical, so feedlot, so farmerish. It's like work!

Branding calves is not supposed to be work! It's supposed to be like Christmas! The Fourth of July! Going to the National Finals Rodeo! Not like getting your Army physical or helping your neighbor unload a semi full of salt blocks. Ya dress up to come to a branding. You wear your chaps and your spurs, not your coveralls and steel-toed Redwings. You worry about missing your dally, not banging your head.

Getting run over in the alley lacks the excitement of having a calf run under your horse. A deft jab with a Hot Shot or professional SQ injection does not elicit the same 'Yee Haws' as a beautiful over-the-shoulder catch double hocking a snakey calf.

It's the difference between shooting a pheasant out of the air or hitting one with your car. Besides, it gives your horse a purpose, and you a little glamour. And we can all use that now and then.

STORY OF THE COWMAN AND THE COW

Ol' Dave was calvin' heifers when the thought occurred to him
"If I'd been born a thousand years ago
I'd still be up at midnight with my flashlight blinkin' out
Because I let my flint supply get low.

The mud would still be ankle deep or snow still to my knees
Though now their old time methods seem so quaint.
Back then I'd have to shoosh her in a drafty calvin' shed
And squeeze her 'tween two panels for restraint.

Or use an ol' rope halter to secure her to a post
So I could slip inside and have a feel.
The oaken bucket would be filled with water cold enough
To turn the chunk of soap as hard as steel.

I'd have to straighten up the calf to grab his two front legs
And loop some calving straps above his hooves.
Then pull when she's a'pushin', watch him pop out on the ground
And hold my breath until he finally moves.

Then rub him down with wads of straw and tickle his wet nose
And leave the two together for a while.
I'd stand there in my tunic till I knew he'd had a suck
Then walk back to the cottage with a smile."

It made him laugh, Ol' Dave, that is, as he rolled up his sleeves,
"A thousand years between back then and now.
We might have better batteries, but some things never change."
The story of the cowman and the cow.

2006 AD

1006 AD

DAVE HOLL

COWBOY EMERGENCY ROOM

It has not been a good year when the nurses in the emergency room call you by your first name. As in, "Roll on in here, Lee, what did ya do this time?"

Judy was talking to her grown daughter on the phone Sunday morning. "Yep, I've finally talked your father into going to the hospital. He's in the bedroom now tryin' to get his shirt on over the bad shoulder. Just a minute, I can't hear ya over his groanin', let me just close the bedroom door."

It began slowly and built up till Lee finally had said, "I can't sleep on my left side 'cause of my bad arm, my right side 'cause of my bad leg, or my back 'cause of my bad back." The shoulder had been the accumulated erosion and stalagmatization of buckin' hay, preg-checking cows and roping. He actually started wearing button-up undershirts since he couldn't raise his arm above his head. That worked until he broke his thumb in a hitchhiking accident and couldn't button his shirt.

"I'll get the shoulder fixed some day," he told the emergency room doctor as they were taping his thumb. He repeated the commitment two months later as they were recasting the re-broken thumb. Judy had always been resigned to his reluctance to get immediate medical help. She watched him for years limp and bang around the house always waiting 'one more day to see how it does.' Her friends often lectured her about taking better care of him. She reminded them that there were rare occasions when she whisked him right to the hospital emergency room in Steamboat an hour away. It was the two times he'd been unconscious.

"He hurt his ankle this morning tryin' to rope a sick calf," Judy continued explaining to her daughter. "...corral was icy, the horse went down. He went ahead and finished checkin' the new calves. Now he can't get his boot off...I better go help him. Bye, love ya."

Judy got Lee loaded in the car but about halfway to Steamboat, he decided he better cut the boot off. She pulled over and came around the passenger side to help. He handed her his pocketknife. "It's sharp," he said, "Yeoww!"

As she wheeled him into the emergency room, everybody said, "Hey Lee! How's the thumb? How's the knee?" How's the shoulder?" Judy had to explain why there was blood and a knife wound in the injured right ankle. They were going to sedate him and had some official questions. "Does he have a church affiliation?" She replied, "If we were religious we'da been in church this morning and this never woulda happened."

That afternoon, they wheeled him out to the car with his ankle tightly wrapped. "Now don't let him put any weight on that," they told her.

"Thanks for everything, I'll take good care of him!" she promised as she accidentally shut the door on his foot!

ONE LEG UP

Jess's friend, Jim was in the army and was wounded in action. A serious leg wound that resulted in a purple heart and a pension.

He recovered and came back to the plains of Colorado and got a job on a drilling rig. Things went well until he caught his bad leg in the kelly and had to have it amputated. Not only did he lose his leg, but he lost his pension. It didn't seem fair.

Sometime down the road he found himself with a wooden leg and a bunch of mother cows. Last calvin' season he was out checkin' for newborns in the heavy bunch. He spotted one whose mama was hovering over him like a stage mother. Jim intended to tag and vaccinate the calf.

Being a practitioner of the 'cowboy mentality', he put on his thinking cap, drove up beside the calf and opened the passenger door. Slick as a pickpocket, Jim leaned out the door and snagged the calf! He dragged it in, but before he could shut the door mama cow stuck in her head and front feet! She started crawling aboard, bawling at the top of her cow lungs!

Jim dove to the left, pushed open the door and dived. His wooden leg caught between the HI-LO 4 wheel drive and the four-on-the-floor stick shifts. It wouldn't budge.

The cow continued to force her way in as Jim dangled out the other side. Straightening his thinking cap, he undid his buckle and fly and managed to strip to the waist (you can strip to the waist from either end) to get free, leaving his pants and enclosed prosthesis still in the cab!

He hit the ground and slithered under the pickup. He lay there panting pantless for five minutes waiting for the cow to leave. She stayed with the calf. He figgered if he could pull the calf out of the pickup, the cow would follow. He reached his arm up from his supine position and palpated periscopically, like an octopus exploring a dog house from under the porch.

Grasping a small foot he managed to extract the calf and the cow crashed out behind it. After they had disengaged a safe distance, Jim slid, drug and hopped back behind the wheel, unwound his pants and leg from the gears and headed back to the house, all the time hoping none of the neighbors would show up.

I commented to Jess that Jim was quite resourceful. "Yup," he said, "He don't do bad for a guy with one foot in the grave."

81

CHICKEN TRAINING

She felt an affection for chickens, she did,
Some might say it was overly so.
So when her good hens started showin' up dead
It dealt her kind heart quite a blow.

The dog, she figgered, that pig-headed cur
That helped the old man with his stock.
He acted like he was the king of the place
The duly crowned cock of the walk.

She laid several traps and kept an eye peeled
To catch the canine in the act.
She'd recently read in the Poultryman's News
Of a cure for these chicken attacks.

The method was crude but was flat guaranteed
To put this behavior to bed.
At last she espied the ol' dog fast asleep
A chicken laid out by his head.

She put on a glove and crept out on the lawn,
Sneaked up and grasped the flat hen
Then proceeded to wallop that fowl killin' dog,
With the chicken, I mean end to end!

He dove for the dog house, she followed him in
There ensued a bodacious uproar!
Timber and bedding and pieces of dog
Came boilin' out through the door!

Over the haystack and down through the creek
And under the black silage tarp,
Leaving behind them a trail of yelping
of feathers, of dog hair and carp.

She whacked him, she pelted, she thrashed him and more
Till the chicken was threadbare and gray.
Exhausted she fell to her knees satisfied
She'd applied the technique the right way.

She loosened her grip on the poor chicken's neck,
A sacrifice made for the flock.
She laid the wee beast reverently out on the lawn
And swooned when it sat up and squawked!

THE TURTLE AND THE RABBIT

I climbed in the cab of the tractor and drove where the cattle were fed,
As a new bride I guess I was nervous. "It's easy as pie," he had said.

But he was a man, what did he know! He could talk about cows and the like
Till people around him would cry out in pain and pray for a nuclear strike.
"To increase your speed push the lever toward rabbit up here at the top,
To slow it just pull back to turtle. All the way back makes it stop.

Okay, he was right, it was simple. I might have misjudged the poor man.
It's just that I'd come from the city and hadn't yet rode for the brand.
I started to circle, no problem. The cows were all flocking in back.
My hubby rode up on the wagon, climbed clear up on top of the stack.

I tried to maintain a good level as he pitched broken bales to the herd.
He was smart and strong and good looking, it's true that my judgement
was blurred
But the scene filled me up with good feelings, my man and the cows all our own
And maybe my handsome prince charming was different from others I'd
known.

When it looked like the load was near finished I pushed to the rabbit some more
And stayed ahead of the cattle who'd started crowding my door.
All of a sudden my husband was yelling and waving his arms!
In the mirror I thought he was laughing, showing off, I admit I was
charmed.

But his antics became more peculiar...sticking his chin in the air,
Hunching his shoulders and cupping his hand like a seal or porpoise in
prayer.
I finally pulled back on the lever, cracked the door and poked out my head,
"Honey," I said in frustration, "I can't hear a word that you said."

"Turtle," he said, "That was turtle! Look, shell," he humped up again.
I watched his perplexing contortions and reviewed my opinion of men.
"If you really expect me to savvy, you should do something simple instead...
Just hop up and down like a rabbit," I told him, "And then...shake yer head!"

85

NINE LIVES OF A SHEEP

Sheep are kind of like cats - you never know they're sick till it's too late.
THE NINE LIVES OF A SHEEP AS TOLD BY AN OLD EWE:

"It all started back when I was born, actually before I was born. My Ma, may she rest in peace, was just a yearlin'. The flock was in a spring pasture, she didn't know skunk cabbage from broccoli with hollandaise sauce. She gobbled the skunk cabbage which affected my two big brothers in-utero. One came out with a tin ear, couldn't carry a tune and the other had a gotch eye that looked at me sideways, all the time. It goes without saying that the herder had to pull them at birth. Forgot about me. I plopped out after everyone had gone home.

"At the marking two months later they banded my tail and ear marked all us ewe lambs. My best friend got tetanus. It could have been me, I guess, but I slipped by the grim reaper a third time.

"My youth was uneventful. I had the normal assortment of lambhood diseases; keds, milk scours, snotty nose. Oh, I forgot, it was durin' that first summer. I had strayed from my Ma to check out some wildflowers in the high mountain meadow. I saw this shadow pass over the ground. All the squirrels and rabbits ran for cover. I froze. Saved my life. The eagle dived but overshot me, whacked his talon on a stump. Flew off with a limp.

"They weaned and sorted us at shippin' time in the fall. 90% of my brothers and sisters went on a truck to California. They thought they were going to Disneyland and teased me for havin' to stay with the flock. Later I heard they got their ticket punched.

"That next spring I found out I was pregnant. I'm still not sure how that happens, most of us believe it has something to do with cottonwood silk or milkweed fluff. Anyway, I had a close call. One big ram lamb baby, I thought I'd die! The herder helped with the delivery. I named it Juan, in his honor.

"Somewhere after the second set of twins I had a coyote scare. I was malingering, in a postpartum funk, hanging around the edge of the herd when I felt something bite my butt...haunch, pardon me. I bawled and kicked, caught that poor sucker right on the adams apple. Made him cough and he spit me loose. I shaped up after that.

"Lately not much to tell. I've had bumble foot, nose bots, liver flukes, stomach worms, pneumonia, been cut every time I've been sheared, had eleven babies, walked a million miles and I'm expecting twins again.

"Lots of humans think being a sheep is boring. Living amidst a mass of other sheep jostling for position. Tramping back and forth on crowded trails looking for the good grass, constantly on guard for the well being of your little lambs. Getting a toe trim or fleece clip now and then and hoping for a kind word from the herder or ram.

"After nine lives, I'd have to agree, it is boring. I might as well have been human.

10 REASONS TO BE IN THE SHEEP BUSINESS

In a recent fictitious survey taken at the International House of Sheep & Ovine Producers (IHSOP) the following answers were given in response to the question, "Why are you in the sheep business?"

* It's the steady income, I guess. We've tried other businesses like tanning salon franchise and firecracker sales but they were so seasonal. Besides, we have twenty sections of sagebrush and high desert south of Duckwater, Nevada so it's not like we're going to subdivide.

* I've always loved animals. And broken mouth ewes are so...I don't know, so cuddly with their cockleburrs, scabby heads and stained britching. Originally I went to college to become an animal control officer but I bought this fleece lined jacket at a flea market in Steamboat Springs and the rest is history.

* The truth is I'm just punchin' woolies till I make enough money to buy the Ford dealership in San Angelo. Truck sales...that's my game. A trader from Mertzon tried to inject a load of goats into me but I said, "No way. These sheep are my yellow brick road to duallys and dollars!"

* Maybe I'm just lucky. No one in my family ever had sheep. They were corn and soybean farmers here in Ohio and you know the compulsion farmers have to mow the five acre lawn from the porch to the road? I thought 'why not use sheep!' So I designed a green saddle blanket for them to wear with a yellow stripe that says "John Deere Model Suffolk" and rent them to the neighbors. Not exactly Thomas Edison but every little bit helps.

* I think I'm in the sheep business for the romance. From childhood the image of the sheep herder captured me. My folks catered to the Harley crowd in Belle Fouche but my hero was the Lone Herder, staff in hand, dog at his side, cursing the flock. Yup, that pungent aroma of formaldehyde footbath or the ringing in your ears from the shearing shed just makes my heart sing.

* Ya know, I'm not sure why I'm still in the sheep business. The market is so volatile. We're starving one year and goin' to Acapulco the next. Wool subsidies, import programs, labor problems, public land restrictions, consumer resistance, cost of dog food, and the constant worry keeps me struggling from one day to the next. But I admit, it allows me to afford the essentials that make life worth living...Maalox, Copenhagen and Valium.

THE LITTLEST SHEPHERD

The night was calm. The sheep were settled in. The dogs hung on the outside ring of the campfire waiting for the three men and boy to finish eating. A coyote howled. Four hundred sixteen ears perked simultaneously, including the 204 sheep. "Better make a circle, boy, before we bed down," said Uncle.

The boy, called Juanito, picked up his long staff, invited a dog and started out in the stubble field. He stopped on the opposite side of the band of sheep. He was scanning their fluffy backs in the moonlight, when he saw a blinding flash and heard a booming soaring crescendo!

He fully expected the sheep to bolt, but they barely stirred. The tumult came from the direction of the sheep camp. He could make out the silhouettes of his two uncles and brother-in-law. Then everything faded to dark. Juanito made his way back around the band to the camp. Sitting on a rough stump by the open fire was a boy his age.

"Don't be scared," said the new boy quietly. "Your kin will be gone for a while but I'll stay and help you with the sheep."

"Who are you?" asked Juanito.

"I'm the angel Floyd."

"No!" said Juanito, disbelieving.

Without seeming to move a muscle, Floyd levitated above Juanito's head. He spread his arms and sang a sweet prolonged note as a bright light glowed from his outstretched hands.

"Chihuahua!" exclaimed Juanito.

"Anything else?" asked Angel Floyd.

"Yes, where did my uncle and them go?"

"To see a baby that will grow up and change the world. Your uncles will become famous because they will be the first to see Him and spread the news. They will be the earth's first Christians.

"They will tell over and over what they saw and heard tonight. They will be revered, sit at emperors' tables, do concerts. They will also be persecuted. The baby will grow and someday will honor them in His teachings. He will call himself a 'shepherd of men'.

"Two thousand years from now the world will be singing songs about this very night. Rejoicing and telling stories about the angels and the baby and your uncles and sister's husband. They will be known and loved by mankind forever and forever."

Juanito scratched a stick through the coals. The coyote howled again. He rose to go, paused and asked the angel, "How do I know you're telling the truth?"

"Angels don't lie," said Floyd.

"And," continued Juanito, "How come I didn't get invited to see the baby, and see the world and get famous and all?"

"Well," said the angel, looking him in the eye, "Somebody has to watch the sheep."

FAITH IN CHRISTMAS

It's Christmas time, when we celebrate the birth of Christ. In the U.S., surveys show that more than 80% of us believe in God. That's more people than have lawyers, drive foreign cars, believe DNA is absolute proof of a criminal act, own a home, have been divorced, or watch Oprah!

How can such a high percentage of a highly educated, well-read, technologically and scientifically knowledgeable people believe in an omnipotent being? Where inside of us is the biological process that allows faith to exist? Not just to exist but to flourish. How do you define the words soul, love, compassion, conscience, guilt or sorrow without going outside the parameters of scientific definition?

To choose to believe only what is scientifically provable is to assume, I guess, that all human behavior can be traced to the basic instincts of territoriality, reproduction of species, and survival. That a conscience is a highly refined sophisticated mechanism that somehow helps keep peace in the herd, insures that each member gets her share of the kill, and that each dog in the pack gets a place in the pecking order.

If Earth is truly just a long series of accidental chemical bondings and adaptation to the environment, and God has no hand in it, then those animal rights folks who say a rat is a dog is a baby, are right. Human existence on earth would have no significance, no more than dinosaurs, rocks, oxygen, stars, wars, or renal dialysis. As Bertrand Russell, an atheist, once said, "Unless one assumes a God, any discussion of life's purpose is meaningless."

One of the dilemmas that deep thinkers have, is the need to explain the biological, physical, neural or meteorological mechanisms that allow something to happen. Miracles are hard for them to swallow. There must be some earthly explanation that the Dead Sea parted, Lazarus rose from the dead, and Jesus turned water to wine.

It is necessary for them to write off Jesus feeding the multitude. To conclude the Bible is more fiction than fact. That Christmas is just a benign commercial day off.

But for the vast majority of Americans, Christmas is the recognition of something bigger than ourselves. It also strengthens our beliefs and reminds us that Jesus was born to change the world and that He has. Our entire concept of God exists by faith. It's not complicated. When I'm asked if I believe Christ was born of a virgin, I say, of course! If I can believe in something so all mighty, all-powerful and unbelievable as God, I can surely believe Jesus was His son.

Merry Christmas, and God bless you.

COUNTRY TRUCK-CITY TRUCK

The country truck was a second hand Ford
three-quarter ton rig with a cow dog on board,
Four on the floor with the right fender squashed
and proud of the fact that he'd never been washed.

"Pee Yoo!" said a voice, "What the heck is that smell!"
The Ford quickly sniffed under his wheel well.
He'd been through the cow lot to take out some hay
and picked up some fresh flavored mud on the way.

He turned to the voice, to try saving face.
A city truck gleamed in the next parking space.
A brand spankin' new Vortec Chevrolet,
a sleek Silverado - pinstriped silver gray.

"Say what!" said the Ford, "I'm a working man's truck!"
"Big deal," said the Chevy, "You still smell like muck.
You think I don't work? You should go where I go.
You'd wear out your bearings and be eatin' crow."

So that afternoon the big Ford did just that.
They picked up some papers, delivered a cat,
Did stop and go traffic, found no place to park,
ran errands and drop-offs till way after dark.

"Yer right," said the Ford, "I'm exhausted, no doubt!
My transmission's achin', I'm plum shifted out.
But just to be fair you should come to my farm."
So he did! 'Cause, he thought, couldn't do any harm.

"Let's go get some breakfast," said Ford to his friend.
They drove to the fuel tank that stood on it's end.
"Oh, I never use diesel," said Chev with disgust.
"It's dirty and smokes, makes my breath smell like bus.

A small quart of oil and gallon of gas
is plenty for me, you know I'll make it last."
"Whatever you say," said Ford, raising his brows,
"Our first job is takin' hay out to the cows."

Which wasn't that easy. The road was a trail.
The Chevy high-centered and picked up a nail.
They changed his flat tire, hauled bushels of grain,
pulled trailers with horses and big logs with chains.

"Don't you have a tractor to help move this stuff?"
"He just does the big jobs," said Ford, a bit gruff,
Just then, for the third time the Chevy got stuck.
See mud is no place for a city-type truck.

But, as we all know there are tough Chevrolets
who ranch and do logging, spend most of their days
With mud on their grill guards and trailers in tow,
plum country-type trucks who can lug it in low.

And city environs are frequently seen
with fancy Ford pickups all shiny and clean
Engaged in the commerce of big city streets
close friends of the taxi, the trolley and fleets.

So Chevy and Ford trucks are different it's true.
But they could change places and frequently do
'Cause city or country depends, not on name
but on the position you play in the game.

For life often picks us to act out a role
as Chevy or Ford, it's beyond our control.
But some just don't fit in life's parking garage,
so you park it outside with the big dually Dodge.

MULE CONVERSION

What makes a man switch from horses to mules...Loneliness? Desperation? Boredom? Something to fulfill his life after he quits chewing Copenhagen?

Deb has watched Jimmy make the change. She actually may have contributed to his fall, which makes her an accessory, because she bought him a carriage for Christmas. She hadn't known he'd been fantasizing about jacks and jennies the same way teamsters fantasize about Reos and Kenworths.

Jimmy started going to buggy and wagon sales, draft horse shows, Amish rodeos. He started learning the names of things, doubletrees, neck yokes, spacers, tugs, sulkies, lines, gees, haws, hitches, hames, contusions, fractures, sprains, bolsters, blinders, britches and bruises. He began experimenting. Maybe it was the challenge that appealed to him...dealing with an equal.

Deb had gone to Amarillo shopping. Upon returning, her 15-year old son, Will, met her at the door. She could tell something was wrong. "Dad's had a small wreck." he said.

"He tried four up, didn't he?" she asked. Will nodded.

"Which ones did he use?"

It turned out Jimmy had hitched George and Huey, two year old mules weighing about 700 pounds each, with Dolly and Patsy, full grown, well broke mules at 1,500 pounds each, to a big rubber-tired flatbed hay wagon. Jimmy wasn't exactly sure which pair should be in front, so he put the big broke mules as the lead. As Custer would say, "I didn't know."

Jimmy didn't have a complete set of harnesses for 4-up, so he improvised with doubled-over baling wire, hay twine, old saddle parts, an inner tube, hog rings, an elevator belt, u-bolts, waterskiing tow rope, and the frayed electrical cord off a broken belt sander. He showed son Will how to work the brake and admonished him to never jump off.

With Jimmy ahold of the lines and young Will with a death grip on the brake, they eased out into the pasture. The jury rigged chains on the wheel horse doubletree began slappin' and bangin'. It spooked the young mules. Jimmy, who had never driven 4-up was still tryin' to get the eight lines sorted out. He looked like a man rassling an octopus. Dolly and Patsy took advantage and were soon pounding across the soft ground like thundering buffalo! George and Huey were trying to keep up. Will was mashing on the brake with all his might and Jimmy was shouting "DON'T JUMP OFF! DON'T JUMP OFF!" They ran until the young mules simply quit, and started dragging their feet. They plowed to a stop with George and Huey sort of wadded up against the wagon.

Thanks to Ace Reid, the patron saint of cowboys, neither mule nor man was hurt except for the blisters between Jimmy's fingers and Will's dog, who sprained an ankle jumping from the wagon at full speed.

Deb says that Jimmy's next major project will be a 20-mule team hitch. Right now he's savin' up hog rings and balin' wire. Should be good. I just hope the dog heals up in time.

JOHNNY THE MULE MAN REVISITED

Johnny was a mule man. That is a statement of fact and also the name of a poem I once wrote.

To me, there are two sides to mule people, the brainy side and the stubborn side.

They are deep thinkers mostly because they always feel the need to explain why they ride mules. This creates a natural stubbornness because mules are smarter than horses and mule people are indignant that everyone doesn't know that!

Johnny liked mules because he wasn't comfortable with horses. He liked to look at them, but I think they were too frivolous, too "fragile" for him. He didn't have time for nuance…with animals or employees. I suspect, though he's long dead, he would lump the modern gentle horse training techniques in with "time outs" for undisciplined children, and investing in miniature cattle.

"It's great to become one with your horse, but do it on your own time!"

He liked to buy mules for the sheep camp. They were not always well-broke. That didn't faze him. He counted on the Basque sheepherders to be tougher than the mules, not more clever, or stronger, or even smarter, just tougher. He was Basque himself and knew how tough they were. Mentally tough, confident, stubborn, belligerent, hard headed, mulish… you get the idea.

But he also had a genius for seeing through the smoke and obstacles of a problem. One year we needed a large number of cows for newly acquired ranches. In spring the feedlots were full of cattle. He told me to breed ALL the light feeder heifers in the feedlot. He didn't tell me how, he just said, "Do it!"

I did. 60 rented Angus bulls, + 30 days, + 1250 heifers, + 62% conception equals, the longest six weeks I ever spent calving heifers!

Johnny didn't visualize the process but he could see the goal. He left the "how to" and the "details" up to those of us who worked for him. It was an excellent training ground for someone who would someday be trying to make a living as a cowboy poet. Particularly since it is illegal to publish poetry in the United States.

The life lessons I learned from Johnny the Mule Man were: 1) How to win the game when you don't know the rules. 2) How to find your way when you don't have a map. And, 3) When someone tells you it can't be done, what they mean is 'they can't do it.'

A TURKEY'S THOUGHTS AT THANKSGIVING

A turkey's thoughts at Thanksgiving.

"I always thought I'd do more with my life. Become a writer, maybe. But it was hard to hold a pencil, I couldn't find a typewriter with the turkey alphabet, it only has 5 letters counting the double B, and it didn't seem right to use a quill.

Like any young polt I entertained the idea of becoming a fireman till I found out I was flammable.

As I matured I became active in worthy causes like "Free Tom", and the Turkey Anti-Defamation Society and The 2 Kilometer Turkey Trot to benefit the Dumb Friends League, in which turkeys outnumber cows, the next largest species, by 100 to 1.

I painted signs for the Turkey Illiteracy Foundation. Which was sort of foolish 'cause nobody could read 'em and I couldn't write. I just drew pictures of turkey's looking at pictures. And, of course how could I forget the Anti-Subway Sandwich protest. We held a sit-down strike in front of the local Subway till most of us got run over.

I went through the snood and wattle piercing phase. We thought it looked cool. Then our apartment manager put a band around our ankles. You talk about being decked out. We could rattle when we strutted our stuff.

But it all went by so quickly and now I'm in the prime of life. I look at my contemporaries. We're all grown and have big plans. I've been working on an International Turkey Olympics, maybe hold it in Ankara. With events like Head Bobbing, Track Leaving, Egg Laying for weight and distance.

Lots of people don't give much thought to a turkey's point of view. They just assume we spend all day gobbling at each other, eating bugs and staring into space. In my case I spend most of my time trying to think. Anything, just trying to think anything. When I put my mind on it sometimes I get an idea, as you can tell. The hard part is trying to remember it.

Did I mention politics? I know some may believe there are already too many turkeys in office; but I think I might have a chance. If I can just establish residence in Florida.

Oh well, people are talking about Thanksgiving. Everybody's goin' home for the holidays. Turkeys are a big part of it, I'm told. I'm not sure exactly what it is we do. But I hope we do it well and that our contribution is appreciated."

ROLLING ROUND BALES

Bareback bronze boys black with dirt and glistening with sweat on the back of a flatbed trailer on a hot, humid summer afternoon, used to be a common sight in rural America.

Putting up hay was steady employment for generations of teens, back when backs were strong, labor was honorable for kids, and a dollar had value.

But things have changed.

Just like the cotton picker, the drive-through car wash and self-serve gas pumps, the round baler has put legions of young men out of work. Maybe that's not quite fair. The kids are now competing for fast food jobs because the farmer and his wife can 'do it all' with machinery. I am not bemoaning this labor saving technology. I never did like stacking baled hay...I still don't. I'm just illustrating the fallout of progress.

To properly handle 1200 lb round bales and giant square bales requires the proper equipment. And because some farmers live on that ragged edge between 'the old days' and 'the new ways,' they are forced to improvise. In an effort to cut costs, Arnie decided to buy one big square bale from his neighbor. It saved him money and would last several weeks. He only had a few sheep, a couple show steers and a horse to feed.

Arnie actually built a small open-sided shed to cover the bale. He welded the frame out of 3" pipe and attached several pieces of used tin for the roof. He built a little dirt berm around the base to keep out water. The four corner posts were cemented in the ground.

The obliging neighbor loaded a 1700 lb bale of alfalfa hay in the bed of Arnie's pickup and sent him home. Arnie backed up under his new one-bale hay shed, and using a roll of baler twine, 2 nylon ropes, a leather strap, an inner tube and 15 feet of log chain, he secured his load to the back left-hand corner pipe. Behind the wheel he let the clutch out. The tires only spun. The truck never moved. So, he dropped into 4-wheel drive, popped the clutch and pulled the entire structure down on top of his pickup!

Blaine, on the other hand, managed to get 2 round bales of meadow hay on back of his one-ton flatbed. He hauled his load home and backed down the slight incline to his barn door. Then he walked around behind, lifted the tailboard and was immediately run over by the bale, which rolled out, knocked him down and flattened him into the gravel.

He said it actually hurt less when the second one came.

THESE BOOTS

My life has been populated with all types of people. This is dedicated to one of the most colorful, helpful, educational, tireless, patient, persistant and irritating professional groups that I have had the priviledge of knowing . . . the salesman. They have made me a better vet, comic, public speaker, and after hours philosopher.

These are the boots of a salesman, specifically an ag sales rep. And they've taken me a million miles sellin' to people who feed the world.

Which makes me part of somethin' good, somethin' bigger than myself. Everybody's good at somethin'; farmers, vets, cowboys, dairymen...and me? I can sell. I can sell rubber boots to a Bedouin, sunglasses to a mole. I can talk my way up from a C+ to a B-.

People buy from people, especially in our business. Which places the obligation on me to deliver what I promise and be there after the sale. My company has to be there for me, too, and it's my duty to ride for the brand.

Somethin' else these boots are made for - waiting...in the milk barn, the feedlot office, the shop, the vet's waiting room or the mud porch. A good salesman has patient boots.

I'll let you in on a secret - these boots love the road! That's hard to explain to your family and friends. But each trip is a fresh start, a new day. Travel lets you put the grumpy clients, snarly sales managers, late expense reports and last weekend in the trade show booth out of mind. The miles give you time to formulate your plan for the next sale. If you could only be as good with the customer as you are in the front seat of your car!

So here I sit waiting for my next appointment, flyers in hand, elbows on knees, boot toe tappin', tickin' like a 2 dollar watch, tuned and ready to put it all on the line one more time, and I'm bettin' on me.

Yup, these boots fit me just fine.

RING BUYING

We had been making the rounds of jewelry stores in search of an item to secure my position as 'good husband.' Mostly I was standing around watching solicitous salespeople hover over my wife the way my dogs flock around me when I walk outside with a plate of scraps.

Mall jewelry store employees dress a little snappier than the average supermarket clerk. Some even tend to the odd, avant-garde or punctilious. I assume this is where Elton John started.

A piercing is not uncommon but it's always tasteful. You never see a salesperson with a javelin through his eyebrow or a piece of turquoise the size of a road apple stuck to her nose. Usually the only tattoos you notice are the discreet flowers, arrows or sunrises on the small of their backs when they squat down. I keep waiting for one of the tattoos to read, "Honk if you love Brittany!"

Suffice it to say it is not a place where a cowboy is right at home.

I found myself muttering non-specific comments to queries like, "Do you like this one?" "Isn't this perfect?" "Do you prefer the 2 carat flawless Marquise in white gold or this throwaway 1/10 carat round cut with the visible bubble and fragment of coal mounted in a copper band that turns your finger green?" Bite yo tongue!

A customer approached me and asked, "Do you think this looks feminine?" He was a robust young man with pink cheeks, the kind of hair that only gets combed when you go to town, and wearing his best pair of work boots. The ring was quite dainty on his big hand. It had three diamonds and lots of curly-que engraving.

"Do you ever plan to wear it?" I asked diplomatically as his mother eyed me.

"I'm getting married," he said.

"Are you an accountant or architect or jewelry store clerk...or do you do outside work?" I asked.

"I'm a hockey player," he answered.

"So you need a ring that comes off easy," I showed him my knuckles. "Cause you don't want to be hangin' that ring on a ladder, barb wire, table saw, or a goalie's front teeth! A breakaway disposable one made of biscuit dough or rubber bands would be best, but they're hard to find,"

I suggested he get something wide without sharp edges, no stones, nothin' stickin' up and wear it only when he wasn't going to be changing the fan belt, cutting grain, ropin' calves or pushing pucks.

"Can I see yours?" he asked.

I showed him.

"Do you like it?" he asked.

I said, "I'm not wearin' it for me."

PAWN SHOP PINUP GIRL

She stood out from the guns and knives and other pawn shop treats
Like a head of Iceberg lettuce in a sea of sugar beets.
It was then I pledged allegiance to what set my heart a'whirl,
Twas a pistol packin' poster of a pawn shop pinup girl.

I don't know what piqued my interest, but perhaps it was that pose
In her gunbelt bandoleras, breathing gunsmoke up her nose.
A blond bombast of bullets with a heart of gold beneath
Like Hemmingway or Roosevelt, a rose between her teeth.

'Calm ye down!' I bade my urgings, Wonder Woman was not real.
She was just the dream of some poor fool's imaginary zeal.
Yet before me blazing brightly with her hands upon her hips
She stared down from an eagle's nest, a feather on her lips.

She had a little smile with a quizzical appeal
That either said, "Come closer," or "Cut the cards and deal."
It's a look that men have pondered since Eve came out of her shell.
Lancelot got lost in Guinevere's, Pancho Villa knew it well.

Poor fools down through the ages, be they kings or pimply teens
Have spent their lives and fortunes in pursuit of what it means.
Thus, she held me with those eagle eyes, as sure as with a sword
That pierced my heart and pinned me to her bug collection board.

Where I sit, today, a captive of her Mona Lisa guile
With her hammer cocked and ready, and her lever-action smile.
'Cause I've hocked my last resistance to temptation in this world
For a pistol packin' poster of a pawn shop pinup girl.

LEBKUCHENS ON THE TRAIL

Every Christmas, as regular as an insulin shot we receive one of my favorite annual gifts. 16 square feet of Lebkuchens. My mother-in-law manufactures these unusual cookies in her garage or possibly in her metallurgy studio. I've never asked about the recipe or the cooking directions.

I assume she uses a cement mixer, pours the sticky dough out on the driveway to dry. It thickens in the sun, then is rolled flat by the kids next door. Once it has hardened it can be lifted like a sheet of plywood and allowed to age like fine wine, silage or Chinese 1,000-year eggs. Since she has no cellar, the sheets of dough are stacked like lumber behind the shop under a blue tarp.

Time goes by. It is a secret how long the dough is allowed to molder, compress, steep, cure, condense and heal but I have seen newspapers stuck to the bottom with President Nixon's picture. I saw the initials BB carved in one like you would put your handprint in cement. I guessed it was Buffalo Bill's.

At harvest time you have a foodstuff that is impervious to toxic chemicals, boiling or radiation, the denseness of an anvil, has the half-life of a radial tire and smells vaguely like licorice and Easy Off. I have seen the table saw she uses to cut them into 2x3 inch squares. It has a 10" masonry blade.

Of course, it is not always wise to examine the process. Like making sausage or legislation, making Lebkuchens is messy. But the result is an addictive, delicious, filling, chewy, long-lasting, floss-proof delicacy you can carry in your back pocket like a wallet, or in your saddlebags.

In addition to lasting longer than jerky, plastic bottles in a landfill, or 7% iodine on your fingers, it can be molded into decorative or functional shapes to shim your welding table, resole shoes, or patch a pinkeye.

Lebkuchens crossed the Bearing Strait with Strom Thurmond, climbed the North Pole with Admiral Perry and were used as a heat shield on Apollo 13.

So, you can see why I wait every year for my Lebkuchens to arrive. They are the cowboy's ultimate tool, to pave with, to sharpen your knife on, to pad your saddle, shoe your horse, scrape unsightly scurf off your elbows and heels, and you can eat them!

My favorite Fredrick Remington painting features a cowboy holding the all-purpose snack aloft as if saluting. It's called simply, "Lebkuchens on the Trail."

★ LEBKUCHENS ON THE TRAIL ★

KELLY'S HALLOWEEN

It was a bad day at Black Rock that fateful Halloween.
It all began the week before, the call had seemed routine.
"I've got a mare needs checkin', Doc, I b'lieve the sweetheart's bred."
"I'll swing by there this afternoon," Good Doctor Kelly said.

The mare was mincing round the stall as Kelly donned the sleeve.
"This should only take a second," his assessment was naive.
"She's just a little nervous, Doc, but...I guess I would be too.
If you were pointin' that at me I'd kick you to Timbucktu!"

Which is precisely what she did. So fast it was a blur.
The next day poor ol' Kelly wore a cast from hip to spur.
With two days off the heal up, his left leg plasterized,
He volunteered to take a call. I know it wasn't wise.

But you know men, like him I mean, a grad of Colorado
whose head, if not for gristle wouldn't even cast a shadow.
Another horse. A small wire cut there just below the hock.
"He's gentle as a new born lamb. He'd never hurt you, Doc."

And sure enough he blocked the site, though awkwardly, I'd think.
He had to spread his legs the way giraffes bend down to drink.
Relieved, he got his suture out, assumed the bent position
About the time a fly appeared in search of fly nutrition.

And lit upon the horse's foot. Just fate I would suppose.
The pony kicked to flick the fly but caught the doctor's nose.
Sideways.
Which left a thumb sized piece of schnoz now dangling from the tip
Like half a jalapeño flapping down upon his lip.

Thirty stitches...on the outside. Then they taped that sucker tight
But them M.D.'s must'uve chuckled 'cause that bandage was a sight.
It stuck out like a gear shift, like the fruit on prickly pear,
Like a big white avocado on a chainsaw grizzly bear.

He stayed at home the next two days hibernating in his cave
Until his wife had asked his help. The instructions that she gave
were "Pick the kids up right at nine at Johnson's, Second Street.
They're at a party, Halloween. Maybe you could Trick or Treat."

"Very funny," Kelly fumed. But when nine o'clock came around
He wedged his cast into the truck and drove himself to town.
When they let him in the Johnson's house he matched the decorations.
The kids all froze. Then screamed in fear and heebie jeebie-ations!

"The mummy! No, it's Frankenstein! It looks so realistic!"
With crutch and cast and nose and scowl it dang sure was sadistic.
But the scream that topped the evening off was, in Mr. Johnson's view,
When he grabbed and jerked the bandage off and said, "Hey, I know you!"

REUNION OF THOSE WHO DARED

I know it can't last forever
But, we made it one more round
Busted up, limpin' some,
A reunion of the lost and found.

Who said you can't live life over,
Who said you can't bring back the past.
Who said you can't relight the eternal flame
Of the memory and make it last.

Gosh, it was great while it lasted.
Nobody could ride'em like us.
Like rockets on fire we shot for the moon
It was win or die tryin' or bust.

We threw ourselves into the melee.
We stayed up all night makin' hay.
We lived our life up to the fullest
Then borrowed against the new day.

We fell in the groove like ol' pardners
Who had one another down pat.
We knew every lick, every turn in the road
Every trap door and tip of the hat.

We brought ourselves back from the ashes,
Set Phoenix's tail on fire,
We reran the race for old time's sake
And finished it under the wire.

So don't tell me it can't last forever
'Cause where there's a will there's a way
But, in fact forever don't matter
Much as makin' it last one more day.

BEHIND THOSE EYES

Behind those eyes there shines a light
That's guided me from my first step
Down life's highway through thick and thin
So I could tell the wrong from right.

Behind those eyes there beats a heart
That taught me love is what you feel
And to be taken as it is
And not something you take apart.

Behind those eyes there lives a soul
That speaks to me from deep within
And warns me I must not despair
Those things in life I can't control.

Behind those eyes there is a love
That never lets me out of sight
And stretches from my deepest flaw
And reaches to the stars above.

Behind those eyes I see myself
The hopes and dreams she had for me
I see myself as I could be
Behind my mother's eyes.

GRANDPA'S WISDOM OF THE AGES

Grandpas have a special job and have since days of yore
To teach his children's children things their parents might ignore.
Like how to spit and whistle, carve initials on a tree
The value of an empty can and why some things aren't free.

Why dogs get stuck, how birds can fly, why Grandma's always right
And how to tie a square knot and the time to stand and fight.
And, if Grandpa is a cowboy and the kid is so inclined
The horn of wisdom empties out to fill his little mind.

He has the kid upon a horse as soon as Mom allows
And fills him full of stories 'bout the old days punchin' cows.
And how when he was "just your age" he rode the rough string snides
And never hesitated, see, that's how he learned how to ride.

So when the horse the kid was ridin' tossed him to the ground
The Grandpa said, "Now get back on, don't let him keep you down."
The boy balked but Grandpa knew the lesson to be learned
"One of us must ride this horse," he said, his voice stern.

Then wisdom passed from old to young, "Yer right," the kid said true,
"You want I let the stirrups out . . . just one hole or two?"

SALMON MOUSSE

The scene at the emergency room was right out of E.R.! But it was not a 4-car pile up, a Metamucil overdose, or a hippopotamus attack, no. Six women, aged 41 to 62, were admitted with food poisoning.

The woman in charge, who had also been the hostess of the Women's Bridge Luncheon Party had sent out invitations. She planned on serving a salmon mousse, vinagarette salad, cold asparagus spears a'la Miracle Whip, with Kit Kats and coffee for dessert.

Lunch had gone well. All the guests had eaten their salmon mousse. The hostess had been worried since the salmon was farm raised, but it was three times cheaper.

She had used the good tablecloth because the luncheon protocol prescribed dresses. After the entrée the hostess cleared the table and went into the kitchen to prepare the Kit Kat cup and coffee. There was the cat up on the counter eating the salmon. Three seconds later the furball was pitched out the screen door.

After dessert, our hostess took the dessert bowls into the kitchen. Glancing out on the porch she saw the cat. It was flat, eyes glazed and tongue lolling. It was dead, poor thing. She panicked! Oh no, the salmon was tainted! It killed the cat!

She gathered up the ladies, their purses, hats and gloves. They loaded in two cars and raced to the hospital! She even remembered to take the suspect salmon for lab tests. Six ladies sat around the emergency room with buckets between their legs and were given emetics orally. In a few moments they were nauseous, gagging and vomiting the masticated mousse, acidic salad, gnawed up asparagus and Kit Kats.

The trip home was dismal. Eventually all the guests were dispersed and our hostess walked into the kitchen. She was still queasy, her hair a mess and she was mortified.

Her neighbor knocked on the screen door. "I'm sorry," he said, "but you were in the middle of your luncheon and I didn't want to disturb you, so I laid your cat here on the step. As I backed out to go to work, I ran over him!"

MASTERCARD - PRICELESS

Mastercard has a very touching ad campaign they call "PRICELESS." For example:

A dozen roses - $19.95

A diamond ring - $2,300.00

The answer "yes" - priceless

One of my friends is always on the lookout for an easy dollar. He suggested we think of some 'priceless' ads that would appeal to the cowboy crowd. Then we could sell 'em to Mastercard and retire. Here's what we came up with:

A brand new super cab dually with a 3 horse slant - $54,650.00

Two AQHA trained horses - $29,905.00

1 team penning buckle - priceless

-or-

A four year old registered purebred Limousin cow - $4,500.00

Nine months feed and upkeep - $295.00

A healthy full term bull calf sired by your neighbor's wanderin'corriente/holstein-cross named Elvis - priceless

-or-

A set of Crockett spurs - $139.00

A bull rope - $65.00

A broken arm - priceless

-or-

A successful Cesarean section on a mama cow - $190.00

A 110 lb healthy calf - $400.00

A missing pair of forceps - priceless

-or-

Complete set of horseshoeing tools including anvil - $680.00

Book on "How To Shoe Horses" - $9.95

A horse who leaves tracks like the intersection of a drill team's figure eight - priceless

-or-

A pair of Paul Bond boots - $600.00

A Bailey hat - $325.00

The 2 1/2 lb petrified wood bolo tie handmade by your retired father-in-law - priceless

-or-

15 years of doing without, working 12 hour days and reinvesting - $901,650.00

A ranch, a cowherd, a family - $3,650,720.00

An endangered mollusk discovered in the one bog you left for the ducks - priceless

-or-

3 1/2 years of fun and playing around in college - $36,000.00

6 years of team roping, horse trading and farriery - $296.00

Marrying a woman with a good job and a Mastercard - priceless

LAZARUS AND THE OWL

Over the years I've become accustomed to the incongruous sight of rugged ranching families, with their weathered faces, rough hands, fearsome pickups and macho confidence, carrying a small dog. A wee dog, a mini-mutt, a pocket poodle.

These petite pups look out of place amongst the bullying cowdogs, big tires and steel shod hooves that make up the rancher's daily environment.

But let me assure you, most of these miniature dogs are tough as a railroad spike. The selective breeding required to shrink these breeds has concentrated certain traits like toughness. Unfortunately it also often concentrates the yipping, snarling, nipping, whining, irritating, egotistical genes as well.

Which brings me to Concho, a toy poodle, beloved by his mistress Georgi, and generally despised by the rest of her family, all her friends and even most of the strangers they meet. Because, of course, Concho accompanies her everywhere they go.

Upon arriving at the home ranch after a weekend of rodeoing, Concho leapt from the truck and played outside while the folks unloaded. An hour later he had disappeared. For two days, Concho remained missing. Wednesday morning found Georgi alone in the house when she heard a scratching at the door. Concho looked up at her and cocked his head as if to say, "How could you, my faithful servant, have let this happen to me!"

The veterinary examination showed no broken bones but lots of swelling and several deep puncture wounds on the back and neck. The vet said the injuries conformed to the pattern of talons on a giant horned owl, but the vet could not understand how he escaped.

Georgi figured she knew how. No sooner had the owl snatched him from the yard and started upward, Concho, true to form, started his yipping, snarling, nipping and whining routine, probably demanding to be treated like the first class passenger he was. The owl raised a leg mid-flight and looked at the nasty little beast screaming dog obscenities and decided something this evil must taste bad and dropped him from the sky!

Concho's still tough and though he's begrudgingly admired, he is still universally despised which suits him fine as long as Georgi waits on him hand and paw. However he's now known by many as Lazarus, as in, 'Georgi, tell us the story of Lazarus and the owl.'

ELK SCENT

Brent epitomizes the typical Montana outdoorsman - a hunter, a cowboy, and conservationist. Hunting season, he and his equally capable wife Kathy had hauled their horses to a camp at the end of the road and prepared to begin the morning bow hunt. Brent had prepared thoroughly, including putting a dollop of concentrated elk urine (aka scent) into a plastic bag along with his cammo hunting clothes to steep overnight.

He placed his compound bow on the hood of the pickup. Several 30" 4-blade razor point arrows were attached to the bow. Ben Gay, his good 12-year old grulla gelding was saddled in anticipation. Brent doused his cammo gear in elk urine. Its pungency stung the eyes of small mammals and made knotholes water.

Kathy stayed upwind ahorseback...Brent swung aboard Ben, picked up his bow and turned his horse downwind.

The full force of the elk urine bouquet enveloped Ben Gay's head. He reacted as if a real bull elk had just walked up behind him and blew into his ear. He started bucking! (Kathy said crow hopping.) They were bucking down a grade, the bow and arrow flapping like a broken wing.

At the bottom of the hill Ben leaped over a giant log! On impact Brent cartwheeled over the front, breaking bones!

Kathy called Duane, the local veterinarian who was the only one who could find the remote location of their camp. Brent said between clenched teeth to bring a stretcher.

It took Doc an excruciating hour to reach them in his Explorer. He had no stretcher but had brought a 5-foot steel small animal exam table. The fifteen miles of Forest Service road were particularly uncomfortable for the 6'7" Brent on the 5' stretcher wedged in the Explorer. Once on the blacktop Dr. Duane kicked his rig up to 95 mph with the windows down and a scarf over his face. The gale force winds helped alleviate the poisonous effect of elk urine that now permeated the cockpit.

Of course, they were stopped by the Montana Highway Patrol. As soon as the officer leaned up to the driver's side window, he was hit by the rolling waves of odor that melted the brim of his hat, pitted his sunglasses and turned his brass cartridges green. He staggered away. Duane left.

The emergency room doctor was a pediatrician and was only able to give Brent a children's dose of morphine. But our hero survived. It turned out that Brent had broken his hip. The patrolman was treated for facial paralysis, Duane had to burn his Explorer, they reported the pediatrician to the ASPCA, Kathy still says crow hopping, and Ben Gay carries several small scars on his rump and right flank in the shape of an X.

GOOSE BUMPS

Emporia, Kansas is on the flyway of the majestic Canada Goose. The cowboys working at the feedlot saw a lot of these big birds. They like corn and silage as well as the steers like it.

Jim is a journeyman feedlot cowboy and was demonstrating his ability with his rope as they pushed some pulls up the alley to the vet shack. The other cowboys respected him and knew that his team-roping buckle was real! Whilst displaying the proper angle and how to control the tip, he lost control, the rope slipped from his hand and shot straight up in the air!

Coincidentally, the lead gander of a low flying squadron of geese heading in for a lunch break flew right into Jim's loop! Honest. There were witnesses. The goose was slapped to the ground like a wayward tetherball. He rose in a squawk and a flurry of feathers, sighted in on Jim and charged!

Jim was riding Buck. Buck was only three, and though he had adjusted to the roar of the feed mill, the claxon of a bucket loader in reverse, and the smell of overflow lagoon, he had never been attacked by maddened waterfowl. Buck swapped ends as Jim grabbed the horn and achieved 0 to 60 in less time than it takes to spell *Pyrocantharincus hyrudinachus*! At the end of the alley, approaching at the speed of a Tiger Woods tee off, was a concrete feed bunk.

While Jim was debating whether to punch the ejection seat, Buck took to the air, and sailed over the concrete obstacle! To no one's surprise, the pursuing goose lifted off the runway and soared between the lip of the bunk and the horizontal neck cable. Unfortunately he was dragging 35 feet of 3/8, softlay, right hand twist nylon rope. The trailing tail whipped around the cable. The elasticity of the steel, the nylon and the vertebrae allowed the feathered projectile to stretch far enough to spring the goose back across the feed bunk like Venus Williams returning a serve! He managed to bounce in a muddy spot and survive.

The audience of cowboys hooted, honked and hollered over the feat of Jim 'heading' a goose. Jim regained his composure, eased the snorting Buck over to the bunk and announced that tomorrow he demonstrates his technique in goose heeling!

TAKE YOUR BELONGINGS AND GO

Across the west this summer thousands of people heard the words, "Take your belongings and go." Drought, lightning, careless humans, arsonists and long-standing unnatural conservation policies combined to create a living inferno of our nation's forests and grasslands.

None of which would have mattered much in the grand scheme of things except that man, a recent newcomer to the planet, has begun to amass possessions. They, these 'belongings', distinguish us from the lower beasts. As the billowing thunderous fires inhaled and exploded, threatening houses, cabins, towns and TV towers with immolation, inhabitants in the crosshairs were told to evacuate. Some had a day's warning, some had a few minutes. "Take your belongings," they were told, "and leave."

It is a credit to Homo sapians that the first 'belonging' most evacuees took, after their families were safe, was their pet. Not the entertainment center, the table saw, the sofa, the swamp cooler, the silverware or the $300 Stetson hat. At the top of the list was Sparky or Miss Kitty. Mongrels with no pedigree, bad habits and a $300 vet bill.

And lest we forget, Fury, Dunny and Bossy were led, ridden or hauled out of harm's way before any thought was given to the gun collection, the Frederick Remington print or the trophy saddle in the tack room.

Why do domestic animals rate so high among our possessions? They are surely not more valuable, in dollars and cents. I think we value them differently than inanimate possessions. The word 'love' keeps creeping into the back of my pencil. But love is not quite right. Responsibility is much closer.

It is long standing, this relationship. Genesis says God gave man dominion over the fish, the fowl, the cattle and every creeping thing over all the earth. Dominion is defined as power over, authority, possession, rule and control. God could have said joint custody, equality, visitation rights, mutual exclusivity or time sharing...but He didn't.

But dominion implies a reciprocal dependence. It is bone deep in our instinct, caring for the flock. It is deeper than love of the land, the house, the car and even the bass boat.

In the face of this summer's fires, "get the animals out first" seemed to be our first thought. In a world where so much emphasis is placed on material possessions, our relationship with our animals turns out to be one of our most redeeming features.

It makes us almost human.

ALPACAS AND CHICKENS

She was an authentic animal lover.

Dee grew up on a western cattle ranch. After she moved away, her suburban neighborhood prevented her from raising cows. "They are so bulky," she said.

But her need to "shepherd" was not satisfied by dogs, cats or even a gerbil. One day she discovered alpacas. They are the Porsche of camelids compared to the Ford Explorer llama or the Humvee dromedary. Any good stockman can affirm that it is possible to develop an affection for a bum lamb or a good and faithful cow. So when I say she loved her alpacas, we livestock people understand that particular bond. But, I admit, I did not entirely grasp the depth of her animal husbandryness.

"Is that an alpaca wound?" I asked, pointing at the scratch on her hand.

"No," she said, as if what she was about to impart was as commonplace a response as "I fell" or "The rosebush got me."

"No," she said, "I got it bathing a chicken."

"I raise hens," she said nonchalantly, as if I could name three people in my entire circle of acquaintances who actually keep layers in their backyard.

"Do they get a bath every weekend, or just on special occasions?" I asked, beginning to question her true relationship with the animal kingdom.

"No, don't be silly. Etta, she's named after my aunt, was being picked on by the other hens and she'd quit laying. She was quite poopy."

I didn't ask for a definition of poopy, after all, I am a veterinarian.

"I tried brushing her, then I tried a nearly disastrous attempt with the steel nozzle of my vacuum cleaner. Finally I filled a bucket with warm water and stood her in it up to her neck."

"After some initial wing flapping she sort of relaxed, kicked back and had a good soak. I washed her affected areas with soap..."

"You mean behind her wattles and under her wing pits?!" I asked, joking.

She laughed. "No, I toweled her off, dried her with the hair dryer, poofed her up and guess what? She laid an egg the next day!"

Dee looked at me and smiled sweetly. She had a tender heart.

"Out of appreciation for your loving care, I bet." I said, and I meant it.

GENERATIONAL DIFFERENCES

Yes, Virginia, things have changed.

A twenty-something couple I know has occasionally sought my counsel. They are married, both animal science graduates and still seeking direction. He is a typical ag boy; strong, honest, has a good work ethic with a background in purebred cattle, fitting, showing, and can weld. He's doing graduate school but keeps busy with his Dodge dually and 20' Featherlight hauling livestock from purebred sales.

She grew up running a few gummer cows with her dad, working at the feedlot processing cattle and weighing grain trucks, president of the FFA and won the team penning three years in a row at the county fair. She wears the 'Top Cowhand' buckle with pride. She's working at a feed mill and going to night school getting a master's degree to get a teaching certificate.

I have suggested since the time they were married, that they would be the perfect couple to run some ranch or livestock farm. They are the ideal production pair...the absentee owner's dream. But their standard reply to me is: We don't want to work seven days a week, 24 hours a day! What is wrong with these kids! I tell them I've never had an 8 – 5 job! What in the world would I do with two days off a week? In a row!

I look at the 21st century veterinary profession. New grads don't want night calls, weekend duty, investment in partnership. They want to raise a family. Spend quality time with their children. They don't want to live 100 miles from the amenities of good schools, shopping and sophisticated entertainment. What's the matter with these kids! Don't they know it's not supposed to be easy! You're supposed to be bone-tired at the end of a day, then do a c-section on a frozen hillside at two in the morning!

I remind them the early bird gets the worm. They say they're not working for worms.

They remind me that all work and no play makes Jack a dull boy. I say to them that dull isn't all bad.

They say money isn't everything. I say you don't work for money, you work for work's sake.

Then they say work isn't everything.

I remember my childhood years visiting relatives in Oklahoma. My uncles were farmers, carpenters, and bricklayers. We would go by and watch them work. All except Uncle Leonard. He would take the week off and drive us to pick up bullets at the firing range, or rose rocks, or arrowheads, or fishing, to the sale, to the zoo or squirrel hunting.

The other uncles chastised him for not having his priorities straight. He should be plowing, or putting up hay, or helping them carry hod. It goes without saying that he was everybody's favorite uncle.

I don't know how I got off on talkin' about Uncle Leonard. Now where was I...?

BIG ONE THAT GOT AWAY BLUES

Their pictures are painted on ancient of caves
Orion has held them on high.
Revered through the ages with instinct so deep
It appears in a young child's eyes.

Since time beyond time they have sat 'round the fire
In the evening reliving the chase
Offering prayers to the heavens above
For the swiftness, the big heart and grace

Of creatures who challenge their strength and their will
To be worthy and up to the task.
But often they fail because nature is fair
But they try, that's all they can ask.

And there 'round the fire small doubts tweak their mind
As they stare at the smoke and the glow
To summon the courage, the patience and skill
For crosswinds beyond their control.

Though novice or blooded, each hopes to himself
That luck will ride with him at dawn
'Cause a second or step in time or in space
Is the difference between git or gone.

These primative thoughts have clouded their minds
Since man started stalking the earth.
The lore is passed down and is part of their soul
They have heard these same songs since their birth,

It hums through their veins. But everyone dreams.
It's what brings them here under the stars,
That primeval force they could never explain
As deep as the craters on Mars.

As the campfire light dances and the flame still entrances
These warriors tradition imbues,
By the glow of the embers the teller remembers
The big one that got away blues.

DAVE HOLL

SO LUCKY TO BE AMERICAN

I am writing this column on my veranda. The heat of the day is dissipating. Shadows are growing longer in the canyon to the south. The bottoms of the clouds are turning pink and the mountains to the east of the valley are glowing purple. Cindy Lou is bustling in the kitchen. I think I smell Teriyaki sauce. My 12-year old is being mauled by 5 little cowdog puppies. The horses are fed. The cows are fat. The quail are chuckling and dusk is waiting in the wings.

As I take a sip of my icy beverage and relax I remind myself of my New Year's resolution; to stop once a day and remind myself that this is as good as it gets. But as that thought sinks in, I become fully aware of how many have given so much so I could be right here. "Right here" for me is to be an American.

Lucky enough to be born in a country where I am free to worship God, free to better myself as best I'm able. Lucky enough to be born in a time when the knowledge of human kind is expanding exponentially, in medicine, physics, transportation, chemistry, extending and improving all our lives.

Lucky to be born while prejudices are fading, poverty is constantly having to be redefined, and America's light continues to shine as a ray of hope for the less fortunate worldwide. But the reality of the debt I owe comes home to roost every day in the papers when I read the names of those soldiers killed in the war on terror.

Every one of them is directly responsible for the freedom I enjoy. They are each one part of a long line of Americans from all walks of life; soldiers, civilians, policemen, firemen, CIA, research scientists, inventors, ministers, teachers, legislators and parents who have sacrificed, toiled, sweated and believed in what America stands for and put their money where their mouth is, whether it's carrying a gun, a stethoscope or flowers to the nursing home.

I owe George Washington, Bill Gates, Grandpa Tommy, Lewis & Clark, Cochise, Federico Peña, Thomas Edison, Uncle Paul, Madeline Albright, Donald Rumsfeld and Pastor Blair.

Two hundred and twenty-some odd years ago a group of citizens as different as Jefferson and Adams or Bush and Gore, conspired to declare our independence and invent a country.

They did just that, like none other on Earth. And that I got so lucky to be blessed to be born here is a miracle I do not take for granted.

I pledge allegiance to the flag of the United States of America.

ABOUT THE AUTHOR

"Slightly irreverent, sometimes poignant and always imbued with respect and admiration for the self-reliance and independence a lot of us from the West are proud of."

-Publisher's Weekly

"Perhaps the most recognizable man in agriculture today is not the U.S. Secretary of Agriculture, not the head of the National Cattlemen's Beef Association, not even the point leader in the Pro Rodeo Cowboy's Association. It is, in fact, a mustached former large animal veterinarian and part time roper who 'just likes to tell stories.'"

-Ark Valley Ag Journal

BAXTER BLACK has been described many ways by many people; as an entertainer, a writer, a veterinarian, a sorry teamroper, Tonight Show oddity, Will Roger's weird grandson, and cowboy poetry action figure.

Photo by Emily Madrid © 2005

How he is thought of depends on how you know him. Whether it's his newspaper column, his radio commentary, his TV shows, as an onstage performer, as a person needing a particular poem for a funeral or, as a neighbor needing help to gather cows.

But regardless of your connection, he remains the same person on the stage in a fancy banquet shirt as he does behind the squeeze chute elbow deep in a cow. What you see is what you get.

As Baxter himself says, "You can't be what you aren't."

ABOUT THE ARTISTS

BOB BLACK

It's a tale you've heard many times. A planet explodes in a nearby galaxy. Concerned parents rocket their newborn baby out into space, where 200 million light years later, the ship crashes to Earth and the child grows up to be the greatest good Samaritan of all time.

Inspired by this story a small farming community inverts a horse tank over a heap of ripe steer manure on which they have duck-taped a child.

"Bill, lemme see your Zippo". A verrrry special child. Who, happily, touches down in the adjoining county sporting minor burns.

A child who came to be known as "Biogas Boy", or, for short, Bob.

BOB BLACK

DON GILL

DON GILL

lives in Gooding, Idaho where he is the county fair manager, chief horse saddler for his daughter Hailey, and Moto cross spectator for his son, Jordan.

When not chasing kids or drawing cartoons, Don and his wife Denise raise bucking bulls. One of which won 2 rounds at the WNFR in 2003. Once in a while Don and Denise get to have dinner together.

DAVE HOLL

lives in the Southeast Arizona portion of "out there," where he punches cows, starts a few young horses, raises some colts, does the chores, is a fair to middlin' cook, listens to alot of different music, reads as much as he can and draws a few pictures . . . his dogs love 'im.

DAVE HOLL

CHARLIE MARSH

CHARLIE MARSH

teaches art at the Haskell County Alternative School in Stigler, Oklahoma. He welcomes the opportunity to illustrate Baxter's stories so he can draw cowboys, horses, cows, and the wrecks that result when those critters get together.

He lives with his wife, Pat, mother-in-law, Vade, a foundered mare, a few cows, a border collie and assorted useless dogs and cats on a small patch about 40 miles south of Muskogee, OK in what a few old-timers and close neighbors call Briartown.

MORE OF BAXTER'S STUFF!!

Want more of Baxter's literary confectioneries? We've GOT 'EM!

Baxter has a smorgasbord of unadulterated, uncut, unfiltered, unrestrained and often ungrammatical cowboy poetry and philosophy in books, CDs and DVDs!

Just go to **www.baxterblack.com** or give us a call at **800-654-2550**. We will be happy to help!

COYOTE COWBOY COMPANY • PO BOX 2190 • BENSON, AZ 85602

BOOKS...

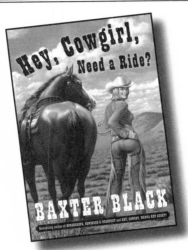

Coyote Cowboy Poetry © 1986

Croutons On A Cow Pie, Vol 2 © 1992

Hey, Cowboy, Wanna Get Lucky?
(Penguin Putnam) © 1995

A Cowful Of Cowboy Poetry © 2000

Horseshoes, Cowsocks & Duckfeet
(Crown Publishers, Inc) © 2002

Hey, Cowgirl, Need A Ride?
(Crown Publishers, Inc) © 2005

CDS...

Baxter Black's Double CD © 1999

Cowboy Mentality and the Big One That Got Away Blues © 2001

Baxter Black's NPR CDs © 2004

DVDS...

Baxter Black's 1st DVD © 2004

Baxter Black's 2nd DVD © 2004